what if there were no titles?

what if there were no titles

aj houston

Not Just Alphabets Publishinig

Copyright © 2015 by AJ Houston. All rights reserved.

Not Just Alphabets Publishing

Fort Worth, Texas

All Not Just Alphabets Publishing titles, AJ Houston, wordart, imprints and lines distributed are available at special quantity discounts for bulk purchases for sales promotion, fund raising, premiums, educational, institutional and library use.

Copyright © 2015 by AJ Houston. All rights reserved.

No part of this work may be reproduced or transmitted in any form or by any means, electronic or mechanical, including photocopying and recording, or by any information storage retrieval system without the prior written permission of A.J. Houston or Not Just Alphabets unless such copying is expressly permitted by federal copyright law. Email notjustalphabets@gmail.com address for Permission.

Printed in the U. S. A.

Library of Congress Catalog Card Number: 099631293-6

ISBN: 978-0-9963129-3-6

Additional Products: by AJ Houston

New Titles Coming Soon
Not Yet Lost Jan 2016
F.A.C.E. June 2016
(Fibromyalgia Awareness Changes Everything)
The Legend of Shrenk July 2016
Lost Pens
(A Pocket Guide for Writers)
all books can be purchased @ amazon.com, createspace, or at the next performance to receive a personalized signature. Booking and contact information can be located on the last page of this book.

Birdie Lee Houston (Mom) and Me

DEDICATION:

This book is dedicated to **my mother, Birdie L Houston**... for the love she shared and taught me how to give... our hearts are magnificent instruments when used properly one man can be an orchestra , a choir or a really really big band. All is never hard to find, she taught me I have more than All if I love hard enough.

what if there were no titles

Table of Contents

(no titles means you can add a title to any of the poems you like)

Introduction	18
_____	20
_____	21
_____	23
_____	24
_____	25
_____	27
_____	29
_____	31
_____	33
_____	34
_____	36
_____	37
_____	39
_____	41
_____	43
_____	44
_____	46
_____	47
_____	48
_____	49
_____	50
_____	51
_____	52
_____	53
_____	54
_____	56

	..57
_____	..58
_____	..59
_____	..60
_____	..62
_____	..64
_____	..66
_____	..67
_____	..68
_____	..70
_____	..71
_____	..72
_____	..74
_____	..76
_____	..78
_____	..79
_____	..80
_____	..82
_____	..83
_____	..84
_____	..86
_____	..87
_____	..88
_____	..89
_____	..90
_____	..91
_____	..92
_____	..93
_____	..94

what if there were no titles

_____	95
_____	96
_____	97
_____	98
_____	99
_____	102
_____	103
_____	104
_____	105
_____	106
_____	107
_____	108
_____	109
_____	111
_____	113
_____	115
_____	117
_____	119
_____	121
_____	123
_____	125
_____	127
_____	129
_____	131
_____	132
_____	133
_____	134
_____	136
_____	138

_____	140
_____	141
_____	142
_____	144
_____	146
_____	148
_____	150
_____	151
_____	152
_____	154
_____	156
_____	158
_____	160
_____	162
_____	164
_____	166
_____	168
_____	170
_____	173
_____	176
_____	177
_____	179
_____	180
_____	183
_____	186
_____	188
_____	190
_____	193
_____	194

what if there were no titles

_____	197
_____	199
_____	201
_____	203
_____	205
_____	207
_____	209
_____	211
_____	214
_____	217
_____	218
_____	219
_____	220
_____	221
_____	223
_____	226
_____	230
_____	233
_____	236
_____	239
_____	240
_____	241
_____	245
_____	247
_____	250
_____	252
_____	253
_____	254
_____	257

_____	...259
_____	...260
_____	...264
_____	...266
_____	...269
_____	...270
_____	...273
_____	...277
_____	...280
_____	...282
_____	...285
_____	...287
_____	...289
_____	...293
_____	...294
_____	...297
_____	...300
_____	...302
_____	...303
_____	...304
_____	...305
_____	...308
_____	...311
_____	...314
_____	...315
_____	...317
_____	...319
_____	...322
_____	...324

what if there were no titles

_____	325
_____	327
_____	329
_____	333
_____	336
_____	338
_____	340
_____	341
_____	345
_____	347
_____	349
_____	350
_____	353

Bonus Verses 355
Table of Additional Content 356

To write is to be and to be is to live... writing to live is in essence what writers do. Discovering what it is you were put here to do is some what easier than the follow through necessary to continue to get better at doing it. There is a battle raging in attempting to write every day, the fight is writing everything presented and not being ashamed of the broken parts of you that will make an appearance ever so often. Thank you for taking a moment to view the messages from my pen. It is truly an honor to display my hearts song in every glimpse or page, in every line formed from living. Feel free to forward your comments to: ***poetajhouston@gmail.com***

BONUS VERSES   **Table of Additional Content**

Appearing here are poems that would more than likely not make an appearance in any of the books I am working on in the coming soon department. I decided if I waited until the next book of poetry, they may not have any relevance to my then which in future terms would be my now. I feel Blessed to be able to write, completely thankful for the gift of words. Your comments are always welcomed.

Breathe	357
Full Moon	359
One More Sun	362
No More Lyrics	365
This Is The Last Time I Fix Broken (1)	368
Thoughts, Words and Dreams	370
Three Things You Must Do When Falling From Heaven	374
Locs	378
Mirrors	381
Dreams	384
I Learned to Say Your Name In My Sleep	387
Note To Self	390
The Word	393
Writing 101	396
In Slumber	399
My Life In Rhythm	402
Lost	405
The Moon	409
Support The Artist	413
Acknowledgements	414
About The Author	415
Contact Information	416

feel free to send your comments to: ***poetajhouston@gmail.com***

Copyright © 2015 by AJ Houston. All rights reserved.

Silence is never golden...
it is the sound of light absent illumination, darkness painted black, it is the sound of NIAP... PAIN spelled backwards. Every VOICE needs to be heard or written. Tell your story, you will be a much better human for the sharing.

Introduction:

What if you had to read something to see if you liked it? *What if you had the option of changing a title to a piece of work you enjoyed, to something you thought described it better?* We take names and titles for granted. We can look up a person on the internet if we know their full name. We can find any book ever written if we know the author or what's written on the cover. Every story, movie, song, poem we enjoy we can find just by its title. Imagine... what if there were no titles? This book... was a third thought-er. The first and second thoughts were to present poems short in length and the longest would be one page long. Only to discover in all word processing programs one page when formatted for print would be slightly longer. I wanted to share my everyday writing in a way I had not witnessed before. I always write and happily place a title at the very top of the page. Sometimes I start writing from using a title as the prompt.

This was a new experience. Each and every day writing has to be a new experience, each poem should leave you with a feeling of relief. It should make you believe you left parts of you on a page or a computer screen. My favorite high school teacher always said *"A Poem should not Say But Be"*... until recently, it was the most profound statement I carried with me to share every day. About a month ago, I purchased a book because I liked the cover and discovered in the contents a short statement, *"in 1950, Archibald Macleish's 'Ars Poetica' asserts" 'A poem should not mean / But be'* – I sat amazed but rest assured astonished at the same time. This taught me the importance of finding the origin of whatever you choose to use in your writings and not take for granted your source is where it came from. I still feel grateful for her placing the words on my tongue. We share so many things in our writings not for sure of its origin, taking at face value the words as a statement of fact. To write something with lasting qualities you must be somewhat certain the core of your data has some resemblance of facts.

The joy in my life comes from working with youth and seasoned writers on the detailing of lines, not explaining the concept of being better at writing; but more so adjusting the way to view the input before the writing begins. I would call it using your poet or writing eyes to see with. To my understanding, human eyes focus more on individual objects, paying little attention to the settings and landscape around them. There is a real difference in telling a story and telling your story. **Anyone can tell a story but your story should have your flavor,** your view from which angle you are telling it. It should be filled with a colorful display of the time of day you are reliving the moment.

'What If There Were No Titles' is my attempt of making poems be. The art of expression is of monumental importance. We share our lives in paintings, in stories, in conversations, in poetry and in new ways we are quickly discovering. I am a writer, I repeat this as often as necessary. It has become easy to lose yourself in new mediums by accident. I wanted to see if I could paint a clear picture, even if every grouping of words were not attached to titles. If I could go away from the usual way of constructing poems and still present connected images. Thank you for your support. It will be my pleasure to hear your opinion of the work included here. Thank you again for supporting art and the artist who strive to get better at Arting.

poetajhouston@gmail.com

what if there were no titles

#

I've been painting again
dripping my broken from pens
unaware of their mission
I got duties growing seeds
angels closely monitoring
the movement of my fingers
I think heaven watches my lips
I got purpose trapped in a syringe
destiny twisted tightly in my locs
I pray in poems
most think are scriptures
worship in verses
there are songs in between breaths
I hear the melodies to
I stop wishing and hoping
when there wasn't room enough
for them to abide in my working
I bled a poem yesterday
it felt good to be rid of it
I get painting and scribbling
mixed up sometimes
they come attached
to the most vivid pictures
mind frames hold
calligraphy's etchings
for at least two eternities
broken isn't easy to say
but it is the whole of me and all I got

#

I have tried to find the words
to tell you what you are
you are the reason
angels are jealous
the reason the sky
cries sometimes
you are why
lonely sounds
so much like love
and alone simply
denotes missing you
you're the reason writers
sit in silence to rediscover
miracles in memories
why the sunrise
and glowing moon
refuse to abandon
the sky and agree
holistically to share
the same heaven
you are sermons on the mount
a parable for healing
a message in a weeping willow
a longing for a weary heart
a revelry of bugles
awakening the dance in steps
many pay for classes to learn
you are the essence

what if there were no titles

colliding my past

with future wishes

you are

closed eye dreams

wearing the aroma

of stay

you are

the quotient

in the elixir

of mathematical properties

scientist are still

attempting to solve

you are

more

than promises

kept and broken

you are

the why

hope creates smiles

you are you

mountaintop beautiful

breathtaking

and sunset lovely

maybe that

is the gift

we should

be most happy

to witness

you

\#

come

walk

with me

my feet

are

conversations

with the

most high

when pressed

together

tightly

our hands

are prayers

I can feel

the blessings

in your bones

when you

hold me

God

told me

to

tell you

his plan

is working

keep

walking

what if there were no titles

\#

she never revealed her tendencies

kleptomaniacs are not aware

they're stealing every encounter

she left with pieces of me

first the beating in my chest

there were days my smile would be absent

I noticed some of my words

were scattered about

only leaving the ones with missing and her

and love and want and her and we

her eyes mirrored heaven

she wore Houdini's hands

must've mastered classes in picking pockets

I think she stole a couple of days out of my week

I only notice the ones she appears in

I wasn't mindful enough

my conscious thoughts were replaced

with images of her

peering at my fingers when I type

she was too beautiful to be thief

to magnificent to have taken so much me

even now I stutter – I am missing hugs

some of my breaths are gone

I think she took those too

I didn't know her tendencies

didn't know klepto's had the ability

to take - to borrow - to steal

me from even me

\#

there is a fail curve

when it comes to love

a test which no one ever scores 100

the fear of loving you

more than being in love with me

is more clock no hands or digits

than sundial buried in the shade

making it impossible to tell what time it is

I find myself lost in moments

in remembering, in laughing

at the way the sun rises

crying at the moon shifting its way

across the midnight sky

I can't find myself at midnight

at one minute past you

I don't know what time I am

one half second early

to my best yesterday

an hour and four minutes past

the late arrival of tomorrow

I've been sleep walking again

chasing dreams of you

around the house

there are footprints we left

in front of the kitchen sink

besides the bathtub, in the hallway

the wash room, living room

carpet still warm

what if there were no titles

from burns

long since forgotten

I don't know what time I am

how many years you were

where we've been - going, or gone

I am not afraid of much

but you haunt me in my wake

open eyes are much more scarier

than open palms

gashing hearts

things I can no longer hold

I have no idea what time I am

what year you are

why missing hands

and digits on clocks

takes me straight to you

time over or over time

again and again

there is a fail curve to love

my teacher taught me

how it works by accident

I must be on the low end

barely passing like time

like minutes, like years

I don't know what time you are

but you will always be

the minutes - hours

days - years

I discover myself lost in

#

she appeared to me in a dream
face familiar, smile the same kind
my mother wore
beautiful, able to rest gently
on the surface of your thoughts
she spoke in whispers
words accompanied by quiet
a soft hum and chorus
song completely unforgettable
she first appeared in a dream
so beautifully frightening
I would pray to never meet her
never let my silence attach to her ears
afraid my eyes would reveal
too much want, too much need
fear my soul would leap out as sacrifice
got me scared to sleep
waking up looking about
I hear her song through fingers tips
whispered in the poems and words
I try to sneak on paper
dreams are sometimes memories in reverse
I met her once - couldn't speak
refused to welcome her to present moments
I broke too much me searching for myself
through piles and parts no one else
felt were worthy of keeping
couldn't wash the gathering

what if there were no titles

of yesterday's off the edges

some parts still reeked of promises un kept

most of them didn't fit perfectly

in the places they were ripped from

she would see the cracks in my pupils

stains of salt on my cheeks

a repaired smile leaning a bit more

toward sadness than preferred

hear the want and so much

need for her in my hello

I must remain silent and bow my head

in an Amen Hallelujah kind of way

thanking the most high for her presence

she mustn't know I'm giving thanks for her presence

she appeared to me in a dream

a closed eye session with destiny

she can never find out she has the look of destiny

the smell of so many tomorrow's in her walk

too much need and want to offer more than hello

I practiced the look away crooked smile

just in case this moment ever got here

I prayed for her never to be here

in my space - in proximity of hugs

close enough to toss my lips against hers

I see the got to in her hands

I must remain silent

she could steal me at hello

unless I keep it

at no more than a whisper

\#

have you ever

loved like

I will need those

clothes you are wearing

I've already began washing

whatever color that is

let's skip today

don't think the sun will rise

there is a 0% chance of rain

let's stay here and wait for downpour

here is the juice you wanted

a few hours from now

had I not kissed you awake

what would you like for breakfast

rest - I got this

tonight will be a crescent moon

we are lying in the perfect position

to see it when night falls

have you ever

kissed like

let's hold our lips together

until they become numb

my lips are fortune tellers

place yours here

I will tell you of our tomorrow's

tomorrow

this may take some time

I heard there is

what if there were no titles

a language of tongues

the way ours move

they must be speaking it

have you ever

held like

you can keep these arms

they would rather be with you

I actually think it is possible

to hold you closer than this

those aren't tattoos

that's the line imprint

of the small of your back

I sincerely apologize

after hugging you once

I've forgotten

how to let go

when told I had

seven wishes left

you - this - embrace

were all of them

have you ever

loved like

kissed like

held like

tomorrow's, the future

forever and yesterday's

were only passwords

to right now

\#

I thought today
would be the best day
to write you a better day
but I can only write what I know
or what I thought I knew
knowing too well
I don't know much
there are things in this life
I am all too familiar with
like how to convince my sons
what I have prepared for dinner
is dinner and not breakfast
or a midday snack
because it is all I could find
in the cupboard and refrigerator
sometimes children mistake
the beauty of love
for pain when it is wet
everybody cries sometimes
until recently
I didn't know this body
held so much water
I know how it feels to struggle
to be the best man you can be
as others try their hand at God
wanting to make you be
the best man they can
we all would rather tinker

what if there were no titles

at being the creator
of someone else
than using
the same powers
to work on ourselves
I know how it feels
to have your daughters
snatched away
when it took them
long enough to learn
mama was only
a voice on the phone
space is not
just the above
undiscovered
and beyond
holding
billions of stars
in place
it's the distance
no matter
how long it took
you to find them
nothing would stop you
from finding them
only to discover
love is just a word
they hear you say

\#

there can be no motion
without movement
no fruit without
planting seeds
or trees first
wishing and wanting
doesn't manufacture anything
there is no progress
without walking
through the process
even our lips move
to make sound
our hearts work because
the body circulates blood throughout
for everything accomplished historically
moving in some direction
was necessary
to everyone who has a dream
goal or purpose
keep running toward it
as though it is the only reason
you have breath
it is up to you
to believe in you
never leave
the most important job
of believing to anyone
but you

#

I never knew the sun could shine
so dark in my days
as though it knows or knew
here, this street - this house
is where lonely lives
never wanted her to stay
not even visit
but wishes don't always come true
there are butterflies gathering
to celebrate my sadness
a host of birds are singing songs
I guess those are the sounds lonely make
lonely doesn't mean you're alone
or together - it could be
time passing in silence
there is a other to lonely
another place, a separate time
a clock ticking backwards to then
refilling volumes of moments, of wishing
I struggle daily with my teeth
attempting to teach them
the story of fingers
they must learn to hold my tongue
you never need to hear
the hopes I have for you
or these noises in my chest
my body rattles when I walk
broken has a melody unique to dark

to the other side of lonely

there are bundles

and stacks of prayers

waiting in heaven

wearing your name

I struggle to learn my hands

to stay closed

fingers to clinch

arms to stay tight by my side

everything I am

is in constant reach for you

I never knew the moon

new my address

it stays full

on my side of the bed

there are shadows looming

drenched in your perfume

the residue of your image

remains locked in my pupils

they refuse to let go

the other side of lonely

is a village

no one knew existed

they say home is where the heart is

I don't know where you are

I will wait here

rest my weary heart

in this other side

in this darkness… until

#

there are ripples in the wind

waves of calm over taking

my ship of a heart

whenever you speak

you become comfort

my thoughts cease

their hurricane ways

I tossed my cares to your voice

to be blown away

I've never been a seafarer

you ocean hugged me

to love the deep

to lay worry floating

where sinking used to be

the only way to swim

love was a shipwreck

I patched the hull too many times

to know some repairs

can't be self-serviced

you rescued me like sunken treasure

as though my soul was X'ed in your spirit

you are garden of Eden fruit gorgeous

the subtle nectar of your lips

could revive the dead

call me Lazarus anytime you like

I'll answer the wind every time

your breeze sees fit

to brush against my days

\#

I bear the scars

of wishing too much

eyes red from starry nights

the memories in my fingers

write of you when I sleep

you just got here

arrival still fresh

planted your feet

as if... here

is where you wish to grow

shuffling my thoughts

as a deck of cards

you are so familiar with

I find myself wearing

tomorrow's smile

a day early

laughing in anticipation

of the jokes

you will tell later

there are bruises

on my skin

from pinching my arms

making sure

I'm not dreaming

my lips has never been this chaff

kissing air will leave them dry

practicing meeting yours is useless

I cover my ears

what if there were no titles

keep hearing

the sound of you

in places you are not

I dream too little

wish too much

neither will

bring you here to me

to now

I don't know

how you got here

my heart was secure

I checked it

for leaks

just yesterday

I wear happy

as a tailored suit

you fit me perfectly

fit my smile

my life

you fit my arms

perfect

you appear to be

the wish

I asked heaven for

at age five

I know this because

I remember

the way you feel

from then

\#

she was a dancer
not openly
didn't club, pole or bar
I could see it in her eyes
the way she walked
there was music in her glide
she was bad er than most
but better than all
I could tell by her smile
her teeth were an orchestra
waiting the perfect director
to wand her song
I practice directing in the dark
wanted to be that perfect
that could make her song better
notes clearer
she was harmony on pause
all she needed was
the right fingers to push play
many tried but didn't know
they had never practiced directing
didn't know she possessed
more instruments than the bands
they listened to in auto tunes
I studied Mozart and Bach
with eyes shut tight
she would learn these hands
these fingers were magic

what if there were no titles

when our eyes met

for the first time

the music started

neither of us knew

how to turn

the volume

down or off

so we danced

her melody

my wand

danced

her feet

my hands

danced

as if heaven

knew before we

she was bad er than most

but better than all

this dance

is what we

were built for

bad isn't bad

if there are no rules

for being good

I whispered to her

be you

we have more songs

to be bad and good to

so let's dance

#

I asked Jimmie

to walk with me

sometimes it takes miles

of moving our feet to listen

the moon set half

smiling on father and son

clouds parted

so we could witness its beauty

there are days the sky

acknowledges listening

clears itself as though ears

can hear their rustling about

I learned from time

fathers can only tell their sons

what needs to be told

only after listening

hearing stories of no never mind

tales of school told from others eyes

laughter has to be included

in the conversation

I had in my poet eyes

their sight sees

more than mere human eyes

could ever scan

I wore my writing gloves

mimicking typing on air

while heaven took minutes

of the meeting

what if there were no titles

sometimes fathers lips
are too big to hear sons needs
sometime fathers ears
with a mind of their own
drown out the welcoming
of new voices
the voices of sons
grow deeper in minutes
sons grow as oaks
in front of our eyes
and we only see the brush
there were few clouds
I noticed but each one
had the shape of destiny
it takes miles
of moving our feet sometimes
when father and son
speak of tomorrows
of school, of classes
barely passing
of love for band
and favorite groups
of wishes – of dreams
of I love you's
I wore my poet eyes
while heaven took notes
I think he loved the slurpee
more than the lessons
I learned from miles of walking

\#

I've been in denial

a supposed drunken stupor

a favorite drug induced high

if love was a drink

I must have sipped too fast

didn't know my limit

swallowed too much you

there isn't a 12 step program

with your name on it

you must be a religion

the way I worshiped

at your altar

my elbows suffer

from muscle memory

they bend when I stand

kneel paying homage

lay prostrate like a prayer

the residual effect of your lips

causes a stagger in these legs

I could never pass a sobriety exam

I have gotten good at saying no

when anyone ask any questions

containing any of the letters

of your name

I'm still in denial

still in search of a concoction

a magic elixir to remove the taste

of you from memory

what if there were no titles

\#

I promised you

secrets

never to tell

how

at first touch

our bodies

became solvent

we were liquid

completely melting

into flesh

I lollipop licked you

as though

you were my first

taste of candy

I tasted you

your river flowed

to my tongue

like it was oceans

I left tongue prints

on every part of you

my fingers

Christopher Columbused

new lands

you had no idea

needed discovering

I kissed your eyes

into rainbows

you said

you had never

rained so much

I promised you

secrets

never tell

how we

sang love

like choirs

with background

singers

hype men

and drummers

dancing to

our rhythms

we melted into

clouds of orgasms

multiple simultaneous

eruptions

you became

volcano

I was

mountainous

you climbed me

Mount Versuviusly

I promised you

secrets

so I will

never tell

anyone how we

what if there were no titles

#

there is a war going on
a battle between being and been
a conflict between spirit and men
to all those me included
who are building something
no else can see
while watching those
you thought loved you
attempt to tear it down
it is ok... your spirit can't be torn
dreams are not breakable
your purpose is yours alone
there will forever be slights of hand
attempting to distract you
a slew of words
trying to remove
your positive outlook
you were built for this
missions are called missions
so you will know
easy was never a part of the plan
there will always be those
got your back friends
you didn't know were waiting
for you to get here
prepare for battle, for war
ain't nothing from this point
going to be easy

\#

the hardest things
to communicate
are usually
things we believed
would be the easiest to say
emotions don't come simple
loving is complicated
our tongues and lips
aren't friends some days
we never have enough funds
to pay bail for words
ligating in the court
of conscious
we let words escape
accidentally
knowing full well
there was so much more
we wanted to
attach to them
before they grew
into sound
keep it simple
is just a phrase
when it comes
before love
loving and being loved
they are all very complicated
emotion filled endeavors

what if there were no titles

#

what if

I told you

we are

the same

and color

was a fence

or wall

built to stand

in the way

of understanding

love is the same color

blood is the same color

dreams are the same color

if we peel

away layers

of misunderstanding

or skin

we would be

right there

in an instant

the same

praying

our pursuit

of purpose

will make us

one

on a path

to enlightenment

\#

I will treat
blank pages
as the prisons
too many adolescents
grow up in
too many adults remain
mentally caged by
too many words
incarcerated by throats
afraid to expand
wide enough to release
every page I touch
are textured steel boxes
a spiral chain linked binding
of imaginative properties
every verse a key to cells
a freedom pass
an unlocking mechanism
to wishes
there are no weigh stations
to hope - just bridges
I treat blank pages
as the opening to heaven's gate
I write not only for release
but wings need something
to attach themselves to
if I plan
to one day fly

#

consider your thoughts or ideas

airplanes or rockets

let them take flight

send them on a mission of discovery

beyond the ground you stand

let them run

far from the complexities

of trials, the constant battle

of mediocrity

prepare the page

let it be a landing strip

or not

maybe they will always remain

unattached to gravities pull

could be there was enough force

when created none of the known

scientific properties

were aware they were here

sometimes we birth giants

in a word, monuments in a sentence

a universe in verses

but only if we give them

sufficient space to grow

If no one told you

before now

you can breathe life into a thought

if you learn

the true function of fingers

#

your pain

tears, loss

and or losses

will directly

and indirectly

enable you

to focus

on the nothing

in front of you

helping you

to build

a testimonial

and temple

out of everything

you have

made it through

reminding you

us - me - we

of why

we are here

find purpose

in everything

even

in nothing

if

that's

all you

got

what if there were no titles

\#

all I need

you to do

is close your eyes

I will whisper

in your ear

conversations

with your thighs

I need to tell you

so it will cum

as no surprise

all I need is voice

to make

your temperature rise

I got verses

that will lick you

up and down

even fully clothed

you can ride my sound

I have lines so you will

miss me when I'm gone

when you walk

your bodies vibrations

will still hum along

at a distance

your hips

will still

be swaying

to my song

\#

there

is

an art

to verse

a pen

painter

of

picturesque

thoughts

a metaphorical

conductor

of

orchestraic

compositions

of words

there is

an art

to everything

especially

the sounds

and songs

we call

poems

#

the amazing thing
about the number
one (1)
is two people
can become it
interestingly enough
when placed in front
or behind
certain words
such as accord
unit, fight
voice, struggle
vision
it multiplies
the volume
of the singular digit
to octaves only
heard in heaven
I often pray
we won't count
too much
we won't
beat each other down
or fight to be
the number
won't hope someone
pins it
on our trophies

or ribbons

or labels us

just so

but we will try

to reach

the heavens

by adding

key words

in front of it

so we can hear

the way it sounds

together

I have dreamed

of

one (1)

before

I wasn't

wearing

or claiming it

or yelling

I am

I was proud

to say

it was sung in unison

my voice

was one (1)

of harmonic balance

of the many

saying we are

what if there were no titles

\#

some days you dance

because you're asked

there will be mornings

you ask someone to dance

for five days a week

you dance

because your bills

demand it

we are all dancers

dancing to music

our feet didn't agree

to move to

what if I told you

inspiration was a dance

of sorts

where music is played

seven days a week

and on those days

you don't feel

like dancing

change the song

to one your soul agrees

to move to - rise

take off your socks

and dance

this is your song

every day play your song

and dance

\#

woke up
this morning
there were
two wishes
and an unedited prayer
still lodged in my teeth
I guess it was a dream
I sent them on their way
my left hand
yielding a ball-peen hammer
my right a thick
rough edged slab of hope
knowing this day
has to be molded
from the beginning
this one is going
to take some time
an sos
a sharpened hack saw
or more focus
than I presently have available
I have so much belief
in these fingers
I know
I can make wings
out of anything
they touch
even you

what if there were no titles

\#

I cannot

make my heart larger

or smaller

than the one given you

can't say more

than what's been said

what is important

are minutes cherished

not time wasted

we can't waste time

someone coined the phrase

unaware

of its impossibility

we can never sit idle

our thoughts are active

even when at rest

we love even when silent

when we refuse

to acknowledge it lives

when we've practiced

stomping it out

love never dies

we label it hate at times

in real words

that is merely love

wrapped in pain

or bacon everyone

seems to love bacon

\#

somewhere in my fingers

lives a herd of wildebeest

a tribe of writers

a host of ancient sketches

hieroglyph's

caring less or more

of what I choose or think

they write anyway

I only share because

they demand

I not keep it to myself

can't tag anybody

maybe a cautious stumble

or accidental reading

is what our mental will allow

I used to be afraid to give

parts of me away

can't grow when I know

these rumblings

don't belong to me

they are on loan or borrowed

I want them to live longer

than the bark of dead trees

I usually carve them on

bones and blood

will destroy paper

much sooner

than later

#

most days

I am inspired

by being inspired

perfectly illogical

but the only way

I can get you to see

the sun is given

to us for light

the air we breathe

a gift from trees

sound all around us

to keep us cognitive

keeping us aware

we are beings

of the same

I think too much

I write more

than that

I sing songs

I haven't

written yet

I am inspired

at the thought

of inspiring

the act of finding

the flame

of inspiration

residing in the

core of me

I believe

we came

readily equipped

to perform

our purpose

when we discover

what it looks like

once you touch

the textured edges

of its existence

you will know

it bares

your name

write everything

touch everything

feel everything

sometimes

if you

slow down

you can use

your fingers

to find

your way

what if there were no titles

\#

I dream

sitting up

fingers

moving

pens dying

from

deprivation

or lack of ink

my tongue

a dream catcher

I kissed you

a proverb

a sonnet

left love notes

on your lips

I used to wish

until I started

helping

heaven

answer

backed up

prayers

in poems

my hands

were forced

to write

there is

a miracle

in here

somewhere

if you look

hard enough

I opened

a promise

in a book

I had

forgotten

I wrote

found

purpose

in my

pockets

life changes

when

you're broke

words

are worth

billions

when

you break

them down

most

will fail

to read

still

waiting

for the sound

what if there were no titles

#

Fact:
no matter what
the answer
to the question is
it will be up to you
to determine
if the description fits
are the measurements
to the garments
suitable
for you to wear
is this in your style
your color
does the cadence
render your feet movable
can you dance to it?
sound is the most effective
form of communication
we have
mostly through our voices
or sign language
when sharing via sound
all the things
we are made of
we are composed of
are translated audibly
write because
you have something to say

because today
was a good day
bad day
one you want to
forget
a day you need
to warn others
not to
attempt to climb
write for want
of knowing
of remembering
of forgetting
of wishing
of regret
write because
you have a pen
a stick
with dirt accessible
write because you know
someday
you will need this lesson
write of her
of him, of them
of yesterday
of tomorrow
write even when you think
you shouldn't
just write

#

sometimes purpose

will shake the ground

causing an earthquake

under your feet

hoping you lose

step or place

determined by how hard

you plant your toes

some winds try

to push you forward

some come to force

the understanding

this ain't easy

turning back

may only satisfy

the coward in you

I stepped

out of the storm

to tell you

your storm

will wait for you

to arrive

prepare yourself

the most difficult part will be

if you fail to come

ready for battle

or believe you have

no need to fight

#

the
epilogue
stated
he had
no choice
but to
love her
her wants
instantly
became
his wishes
her lips
held
secrets
he never
thought
of sharing
some stories
are too long
to make short
too big
to be
tall tales
to him
everything
about her
was
epic

what if there were no titles

\#

when I

close my eyes

I remember you

the aroma

delivered

by the wind

at your arrival

the sound

of your glide

left leg a bit slow

on the upbeat

in my mind

you touch me

right hand first

fingers respond

knowing

my want

and their grasp

are listening

to the same song

we will kiss

as if clocks

know

to stop

as your lips

approach

in moments

like these

time

always

stands still

your left hand

slowly pressed

against my spine

letting me know

support

has come at last

I remember you

you smell

of dinner

felt like

vacations

reminded me

of jacks

hopscotch

and the joy

of being young

felt comfortable

spilling all of me

in your welcoming ear

my cares discovered

your lap a pillow

I remember you

what took you

so long

to get here

what if there were no titles

\#

the battles
are usually
intellectual
fist and guns
make martyrs of thinkers
fighting without a plan
of who to fight
or when to attack
are the fundamental
principles of riots
revolutions are diagrams
with arrows pointing
from here to there
from struggle to free
one can speak for millions
or millions can shout
for millions
the problem remains
how many voices
are too many
to be audibly clear
how many voices
can one person hear
when will we decide
it is time to draw the line
and use our minds
to do more than just
imagine

\#

found

an

abandoned

halo

I

wouldn't

normally

bring

it up

but

this

one

is

decorated

in your

favorite

color

so

I will

keep it

safe

until

you

are

ready

to

re adorn

it

#

every day

I sit here

waiting

writing

wondering

how long it takes

for memories

to forget

they are

memories

forget they

belong to you

wonder how long

sound last

after it fades

and why the sun

looks like

that same sun

and the moon

glows

like it is still there

from the other night

watching me

wish

listening to my

whispers

I keep trying

to write

a prayer

in the language

of angels

maybe it will

get there faster

I stop rushing

words

when they began

dancing

off my tongue

my words

mimic how you walk

I need to pray

to stop wanting

I need to wish

and stop writing

I need to write

these wishes

I need to pen

these memories

I found a pen

that whispers

told it to tell the sun

to tell the moon

not to change

to keep glowing

like the other night

until these memories

forget they are mine

#

sometimes

we lose our way

broken on the inside

outside whole

the challenge is

to realize

you are broken

to understand

being broken

is the first step

in finding the rest

of the fractured

parts of you

to rebuild you whole

no new relationship

can fix it

simply patching

the holes you find

will not work

prayer is good

but that's a repair

my spirit thing

not a complete

fix it kit

we were given hands

because

somewhere

in the process

of our creation

it was known

we would have to

put them to use

on ourselves

we are all

minute men

and women

armed and ready

for next

do not doubt

your ability

to fix yourself

anyone else

attempting to do so

may believe

some of your

yesterday's

do not need

to be included

we have our today

our now's

and yesterday's

locked in the cells

of our fingertips

put them to good use

if you believe

you can do it

it can surely be done

#

when you've been
riding with purpose
after a while
it trains your eyes to see
from a different
perspective
I see you
through the new eyes
purpose
loaned me
to look through
I see that you
sitting all comfortable
satisfied with settling
happy to have friends
that are comfortable
now your dreams
can only
rustle with
your conscious
while in slumber
you talk like them
walk like them
act like them
but you are not
like them at all
I can see
the magnificent you

chained to the bottom

of your tongue

because you know

you are the smartest

in your circle

and your fingers

are afraid to draw

a bigger round

it has been occurring

for centuries

purpose

explained it to me

when we first met

how fear can put

on happy clothes

and fool

the great ones

to walk with him

and be very comfortable

playing games

of simplicity

living in complacency

I know you can feel

your greatness

beating

on the inside

of your chest

I can see it

from here

what if there were no titles

\#

I
dreamed
of you
before
our first
meeting
thought
it was
just a dream
until now
I'm not
saying
dreams
come true
but
neglecting
to acknowledge
heavens knows
more than
we do
when
blessings
rain down
on us
unexpectedly
would be
foolish
on my part

\#

if you listen
to the naysayers
you to will believe
happiness is just a mirage
something you only see
in the distant glare of sun
while on your way
to destiny
when I met happiness
I asked her
of her requirements to stay
she explained
just because she
is willing to meet you
doesn't means
she plans to stay
there was a ferociousness
in your quest
to have her stop by
then you became
lackadaisical in your drive
to better days
so she left
happiness
can be found always
in your surge for tomorrow
not in you patiently waiting
for tomorrow to arrive

what if there were no titles

\#

we have heard
the saying
'starting over' and
'starting from scratch'
so many times
it is associated
with being bad
preferably stated
'not good' or some
grave occurrence
we are too ashamed
to pronounce
what if we changed
the words to
rebirth, new beginning
a path to future success
it will always matter
how you say it
every race
has a starting line
every book
a beginning
every newborn's parents
go all out to celebrate
their first birthday
we witness
starting over daily
and forget

to apply it
to life
we live in
plain view
an open arena
to the suggestions
of others
no one will do
what they tell you
to do
if they were in
the same shoes
as you
the start of anything
should be a celebration
the start of everything
should come with
quotation marks
starting over
only surmises
a new day
has arrived
wake up, get up
welcome it
with arms open
just in the
slightest case
it needs a hug
or something

what if there were no titles

#

we applaud
our nieces and nephews
celebrate with them
another year of living
as we watch them grow
congratulate our friends
tell them how well
they've done
growing their seeds
why is it we
never treat
our dreams
as children
we don't know
how old they are
or know
when it is time
for them to graduate
no one
not even us
will see how
big our dream
has grown until we
let it fade away
your dream requires
you to nourish it
how else will it
reach fruition

\#

if
you
want
to
be
the best
at
what
you do
you must
reeducate
yourself
refine
the process
of doing it
don't be
afraid
of learning
it may not
make you
the best
but it will
make you
better
challenge
yourself
to be
better

what if there were no titles

#

it would

be nice

if we could

choose

who to love

why we love

when to love

or when to stop

loving

imagine

how chaotic

it would be

for writers

not enough pain

to fill a sentence

or not enough

love

to fill a library

I have enough pain

to fill a library

and too much

love

for the magnets

no longer attracted

to this heart

that was formed

out of the right

metallic substance

not too long ago
choice is the best
and worst gift
humans
were given
it didn't come
with instructions
or take backs
or do overs
loving
or falling in love
with someone
is not often
a choice
the best thing
and the greatest
problem
with love
is
love has
her own eyes
hands and fingers
and usually
points out
unsuspectingly
sending our hearts
away before
we even notice
it is gone

what if there were no titles

\#

every morning

of every day I write

without expectation

without thinking

I know where my fingers

will take me this new day

writing of sadness

from my happy place

writing of joy

from the same

I am happy to be writing

I write because writers must

writing is necessary

in becoming a better thinker

I want to better at thinking

I write every day

out of the pleasure

I get from seeing thoughts

manifested into words

just write

you will find the best you

trapped in a sentence

hiding behind

a misplaced comma

caught somewhere

in the middle of

pen tip and paper

just write

\#

if
you
think
I love you's
are
free
ask
your
heart
to
explain
in the
currency
of
memories
or time
there
is
no truth
in
the phrase
'love
don't
cost
a thing'
forever's
are
priceless

what if there were no titles

\#

I was asked
why do I write
of love so much
tried to explain
so many write of pain
my ears were becoming
imbalanced
not that pain isn't relevant
but we only have pain
because we loved so hard
cared too much but who's to say
how much caring is too much
I want to always remember
kisses will last longer
than the touching of lips
smiles are magical
when lips turn upward
nearly ripping the corners
of mouths
love doesn't die
no matter how much dirt
or mud our tongues attempt
to bury it under
we are built of love
why do you think
there is such an outward quest
to complement
our inward being

\#

trees

are planted

mainly for

two reasons

either for

their shade

or their fruit

not one

of those

are instant

you must

nurture

and help

them grow

your best

today

has to be

better

tomorrow

best takes

time

and work

not one

of them

are instant

you have to

grow best

like trees

what if there were no titles

#

most nights

while everyone

is sleeping

I sit knitting

hope a sweater

in the brightest

colors possible

wanting the chill

of day to require

it be worn

I need everybody

to know

hope gets cold too

needs the warmth

of humans

hope needs hugs

needs kisses

needs to know

it is wanted

hope gets lonely

when you think

she doesn't exist

I need all to see

there is always hope

even if

she is wearing

an ugly

uneven knitted sweater

\#

we
marvel
at mountains
many lost
their lives
attempting
to conquer
or climb
many believe
it's the same
thing
truth
be told
mountains
are
particles
of dust
that
understood
and believed
in a unique
concept
of bonding
and
the
ultimate
power
of unity

what if there were no titles

\#

beginning

anything

is hard

sticking

to

anything

is hard

writing

everything

is hard

it depends

on

how much

you want

to

remember

and

how much

you are

willing

to

sacrifice

in

remembrance

\#

some

mornings

whether you

climb from

the depths

of despair

recover

from

the shadows

of dimness

or rise

from

the ashes

of creation

this is

a new day

a new promise

you must make

to yourself

a new sun

even if clouds

attempt to

fool you

into thinking

it is absent

never doubt

the power

of you

what if there were no titles

#

in

order

to

teach

someone

how

to

write

better

you

must

be

a learner

of better

writing

in other

words

to teach

better

writing

you must

be

a student

at the

writing

better

institute

yourself

\#

the task of the writer
is to build smiles
from the broken pieces
scattered about abandoned
gone ain't never been gone
and lost we always find
the last place we look
I have been lost before
found my way by sundial
saved my tears in a bucket
I wanted to feel how
they felt in my palms
there is so much
to look forward to
in a day I have never
shared time with
as a boy I used to pretend
I was a writer - as a writer
I pretend I am a boy
most of your friends
will never buy your books
or read your words
completely
they think they know
the whole of you
do not worry
you don't even know
the whole of you... keep writing

\#

I
chase
myself
every
day
got
too
long
of a
list
to
start
my
morning
walking
as
though
time
and
I
are
friends

#

your circumstances
can never bind you
to any specific outcome
the path you walk
can be easily
redirected with
a simple side step
your today will not hold
your tomorrows hostage
we were formed
from dirt
which makes this earth
ours to own
no journey will ever be
decided or determined
by the street
you start from
we are all
works in progress
as long as
we keep moving
greatness is in
self-discovery
never let
anyone else's tongue
paint you perfect
you were perfect
before you met them

what if there were no titles

\#

if this

writing

thing

was going

to be easy

we would

all be born

with pens

in our

hands

since that

was not

the case

the quicker

you pick

one up

the more

expediently

it will become

the more favorite

of weapons

in your arsenal

and everybody

knows

there is

nothing mightier

than a moving

pen

\#

in hind sight
I know now - what I wish
someone should have explained
at the beginning of this race
I must have forced the word TRY
into the most important spaces
in sentences it didn't have the strength
or potential to push through
if it matters how you say it
your approach has to matter
I should have used CAN, WILL
and GOT TO a lot more
should have redefined IS and BE
should have placed the No Options Tag
on trials and problems to warn them
if need be we will do this dance without music
if I knew the power of words in the beginning
the first line of every verse
would be a flying fist, elbow or punch
I would have studied PenJitsu
instead memorizing nursery rhymes
my favorite pen would have the swiftest feet
roundhouse, crescent and sidekicks
I would have stayed with every Plan A
the path wasn't paved yet anyway
if I would have known every test
wasn't pass or fail - it was pass or go again
TRY leaves too many exits available

what if there were no titles

gives the probability

of turning back

we seem to carry a mouth full

of useless we keep using

IS and BE are the strongest verbs

in our vocabulary

in hind sight - I know now

what I wish someone

had whispered

in my crib before

before I heard

I want you to TRY

TRY and crawl

TRY and walk

TRY to repeat after me

imagine the difference

if my first words were a fist

if my lips were thrusting sidekicks

if I could run before I crawled

if I could jump before I walked

I would never be afraid of snakes

even if they offered me

the purest red delicious apples

I would believe lightning and thunder

were answers to questions I asked

the night or the day before

I wouldn't name hurricanes

after women, men or slave ships

I would just call them hurricanes

we would be cool like that
you probably don't know
can't really comprehend
how a different beginning
would leave you with new options
either a tragic
or a most glorious middle
we are not nearing the end
so picking it apart right now
would make absolutely no sense
I am not saying your start
will determine how
or where you finish
all I know is
you can build mansions
on foundations
if they are built
to hold that much weight
I know some of these dreams
I drag around with a crane
I know now - what I wish
someone had told me
at the beginning of this race
TRY will not get the job done
if you don't start with some
GOT TO, CAN, WILL or No Options
you just wasting time
to tell the truth neither you nor I
have any time to be wasting

what if there were no titles

\#

over

the years

I have collected

enough silence

to conduct

a symphony

of quiet

sometimes

my heart rest

on the edge

of collapse

my fingers

pause

too long

to make

a clear

response

my lips shiver

at the thought

of telling you

a belly filled with

miss you's

could not break

the code of

hush

even if

I wanted

it to

\#

there are stars in the sky
I haven't named yet
waiting for you to pick the ones
you think are worthy
we may never know
the real name of flowers
we only know the names
we gave them together
telling others how we met
wouldn't make sense
most cosmic occurrences
require scientific data
and research to become believable
can't explain how I've come
to love you or define love in terms of time
for love explains itself in time
and time has no effect on love
there are words I want to say to you
I am still carving out of stone
my heart has begun getting rid of
songs it use to love
making more room for you
I have created a journal
of the memories we have yet
to make happen
finally added everything
to my bucket list - I pray
I spelled your name correctly

#

dreams have pauses

not setbacks

come with sometimes slow

never stop

there is no incubation period

or cocoon morphing

it to grow as tall

as you need it to be

for others to notice it is real

dreams don't come

with life cycles

or just in case scenarios

plan B's or a series of options

dreams are actual living beings

sacrificed pieces of you

for the good of someone else

maybe you hid it in a poem

a painting, a picture

a story, a song

a business - it doesn't matter

it cannot breathe on its own

it needs your legs to run

your mouth to speak

your eyes to see

there is no such thing

as living a dream

if you believe in sleep

dreams don't sleep

\#

I
wish
inspiration
didn't
have
such
a
loud
voice
then
maybe
I
could
rest
if
she
whispered
instead
of
always
yelling
in
my
ear

\#

I
believe
our
greatest
fear
is
discovering
the
value
of you
(the inner you)
and
having
to pay
for it
the rest
of your
life
purpose
demands
you
practice
being
the best you
the one person
you can
never lie to
is yourself

\#

when

you stop

thinking

poetry is

in a name

or found

in the verses

you've formed

on whatever

mediums

and media's

you formed them

when you stop

writing poetry

and become

the words

you write

you will

no longer

have to

waste words

explaining

to innocents

what poetry is

you can

show them

what poetry

be

what if there were no titles

\#

everything

you write

should have

a piece

of every

part

of you

consider

it not

sacrifice

but a

building

of the

better you

full vessels

cannot

be filled

you must

determine

how much

to out pour

relative to

how much

to take in

you are

your own

source of

give and take

\#

sometimes we stop time

move on or up or backwards

until we notice

time never stopped

we did

not our choice

but things happen

exactly the way

they are supposed to

there will always be arms waiting

words that can catch our balance

when we discover we are off balance

life is more high wire than street

more stop the hurt than make a wish

I missed you

more than you know

happy you shared your story with me

sad because of what you went through

just to make it back for balance

I will talk of nothing

if that keeps you talking

talk of everything

if that will make you smile

I was at a loss for words

until you asked me to write

to write of you

to you - for you

I will write you

what if there were no titles

if that's what you need
I can't say what I want or think
don't know the answers
don't know what questions
I need answers to
maybe I'll ask
your smile to smile
or your arms
for an embrace
both are worth years of waiting
you want to know things
you already know
I will write sunshine if you
need to find your way
out of the dark
I know what you are
you are beautiful
you are much more
than you know
much more than I can write
in the minutes you gave me
I am glad you are close
no need to be near
when you reside in my thoughts
I missed you
when you were far
close is good
worthy of words
worthy of writing about

\#

I am learning forgive me's
I have struggled through enough years
not knowing how to forget
if I can forgive me
you've already been forgiven
not that you asked or needed it
forgiveness is never
for the person or people
you believe you are forgiving
it is more for the forgiver
my heart is in a constant tug of war
for love and purpose
no space for anger or disputes
we were built for loving
it is easy to forget sometimes
love never travels alone
her friends are as devious as diamonds
she wears complicated clothes
mismatching shoes
multicolored dresses
it is not easy to view her
through her make up
purpose will never tell you
where she came from
or notify you the day she leaves
she wears the best perfumes
her aroma lingers
as slowly as tulips grow

what if there were no titles

these forgive me's
and forgot's
are hard to
sort through
I bundled so many
of tomorrows greetings
in yesterday's hello
I find myself
practicing
my smiling goodbyes
at your arrival
I know how hard
it is to stay
when you are needed
I've watched
going be gone
even when there
is no place left to go
sanity is a padded room
with lockless doors
I find myself staying there
much longer than I'd like
forgetting this world
lost its logic
sanity doesn't live
here anymore
I am learning forgive me's
you can only stay motivated
if you first learn to forget

\#

I've discovered
undocumented oceans
hiding behind the coverings
of my pupils
sometimes I leak a fountain
I have dried lakes before
but can't damn the corners
or patch the pain
love escapes from
I thought I broke myself
believed I ran out of oceans
there are days I drink
more water than required
wouldn't know what to do
if the source ever became empty
I have discovered my heart empty
all of its contents stolen
or given, or taken, or shared
I guess it is more important
how you feel it is
than how it was
all is often too heavy a load
to rest gently
on someone else's shoulders
even if you warn them
sometimes my eyes rain
more than heaven
a contest to see which one

what if there were no titles

contains the most oceans
I've scaled destiny and purpose
they often weigh in
a couple of kilos short
I keep adding nourishment
but they will never
be any heavier
than they are right now
I find myself in places
I am supposed to be
meeting actually
who I am supposed to meet
not that I checked mark
God's to do list
to know what comes after
or before, or next
waiting is a skill
a master course
I seem to fail daily
I keeping taking the same exam
I asked my eyes what are they looking for
looking at, wishing to see, why oceans
why storms reside in their corners
thunder less, give me clouds
winds, strikes of lightning
I'll be waiting
embracing these oceans
drinking more water
than required

\#

this morning
I laid out four pads and four pens
it is impossible to tell your truth
if you fail to include all four parts
I have found the most delicate parts of me
lodged deeply in the secrets
I hide from myself
I am an open vault behind a screen
of multicolored deadbolts
intentionally locked years ago
for safety's sake
then swallowed the keys
there is beauty in the way
trade winds blow
with nothing to offer or trade for
I wanted you to see me
not close enough to know
to touch, to feel
needing is so much more
than wanting
there are mysteries in sound
in the words we parlay
back and forth as bets in a casino
I go all in too often
actually believing
my heart, or these lips
can beat four of a kind
I wrote my truth on each page differently

what if there were no titles

not sure if you possess
the skills required to read each line
the only thing lying between them
are you, I and these truths
I think too much of you
not to lay my soul open
so you can pick what you like
take your choice of caricatures
witness the change of terrain
in the words laid out for you
to walkthrough
I ran out of hiding places
your smile is a playground
don't think I've ever
frolicked until now
or felt such joy in the life lines
of an open palm
I placed me on four pads with open pages
so you could read my story
there are so few happy endings
so much laughter in the pain
so much ecstasy in remembering
I wanted you to know
there is so much
me to discover
If you lay your four pads open
and write with me
we can write
the miracles of truth

\#

this is the fifth time

I've rewritten this story

the ending somehow

remains the same

every night I force myself

to stop loving you

force my thoughts

to erase your smile

from the festival of celebrations

somewhere in my mind

you are the event I parade

there are stilts, clowns,

jugglers and high wire acts

I tell myself to stop

jumping and yelling

standing in the midst of the audience

I know you don't see me that way

I can't jump high enough

to be noticed

my voice isn't bass clef loud

for you to make out

smothered by constant applause

and in comes morning

its rays of sun

or clouds of grey matters not

everything is back

returned as pristine and shiny

as if I hadn't spent all night

what if there were no titles

to un write this story
this is the fifth time
I've rewritten this story
I wake, drenched in memory
clinching moments
that never happened
feeling so much like love
I tell myself to let go
releasing will require
the opening of hands
how can fingers be this disobedient
or maybe it's just you wearing God's smile
as though he gave it you for keeps
he knows the effect
it has on the blind
on men like me
always dreaming of heaven
can't wipe away this drenching of you
in my mornings - can't write a story
of different endings
I will write a tale of woe
of how you thieved the other me
replaced it with this lost one
how this lost one only finds you
celebrates the parade of your entrance
every morning come rain or sun
drenched in memories covered in smiles
of events, of closed eye wishes
that never happened

\#

I used to love writing
loved the sound and rhythm
of a fine point pen
sliding smoothly across pages
until it begin to feel
I was carving words and thoughts
with fingers and bones
there was too much me
displayed for viewing
everything I've written
can be placed back into this body
in the exact space it was removed from
nothing is easy at first glance
you will not hear your own footsteps
you will not see you go
won't be aware of the distance
you will just arrive
wearing a spectacular look of wonder
amazed you didn't feel the journey
love is not a good Samaritan
it will not help you find your way
love doesn't care
if your balance has been stolen
you are left with one choice
loving is not a choice you make
you would believe your heart
possessed fingers or a long arm
the way it snatched your attention

what if there were no titles

the way it ripped your emotions
from the places you didn't know
emotions lived
late is thinking you're early
thinking you have time to change
offering likes instead of love you's
late is attempting to use
human hands to catch yourself
as you fall, when you fall, after you fall
writing was always my comfort zone
until it begin revealing my secrets
I hid them so well
had forgotten how to read them
you will never know
who is waiting to steal your precious
raid the treasure of your kisses
you will not hear them coming
they will simply arrive at your lips
I still love writing
still enjoy the music
of fine tip pens on blank sheets
I arrived with the understanding
too late to know
too far gone
don't know how I got here
or why waiting brings smiles
I guess love makes herself new
every time she finds me
waiting

#

if she could see me
witness how she is there
every waking moment
tiptoeing through my dreams
I would tell her if I knew how
she only notices my sprint
how feet fast I arrive
in her direction
to marvel at everything
God gave her
and damn
did he bless her
I think she still wears
heavens feet
the way she moves
as the earth sings hallelujahs
and hid her wings in her hips
they move as if flight
remains a definite possibility
if she could see me
see my wish list
is merely a map
of all the blessings
God gave her
he said was good
I think are great
I asked heaven for permission
to let me rock her to sleep

what if there were no titles

I can rock her to sleep
I got gifts from heaven too
and blessed to know
how to use them
I learned of flight
from angels
if she could see me
she would know
seeing is believing
and I believe
she has never seen
rocking or lullabies'
or ecstasy
as heaven gifted
us to share
if she could see me
I would tell her
if I knew how
what heaven told me
to whisper to her soul
soul mates
are born heaven first
then there is this
rocking thing
if she could see me
words would need no sound
all she would need
is for me
to rock her a lullaby

\#

daily aspirations of better
will never be accomplished
if you fail to respect yourself
the definition morphs
as necessity demands
she left, smiling, door open
no goodbye
respect is understanding
sometimes goodbyes mimic hello's
sometimes I'm sorry's are just sounds
to shake memories lose
from the base of your foundation
possibly uprooting seasoned oaks
as if the earth agreed to let go
reverberating unbalance
throughout these shattered bones
I thought these bones were mine
thought they could survive leaving
sometimes wishing is futile
similar to a butterfly
fighting against the winds of a hurricane
respect is knowing she stayed
as long as time would allow
as long as her feet
could withstand standing still
standing still is a movement of its own
sometimes gone is here
and leaving didn't know

what if there were no titles

had no idea where to go
didn't know when to leave
I now believe in ghost
I wondered why her face faded
in her approach
I guess staying was part
of a mathematical equation
we were not smart enough
to input the right numbers
I counted the good mornings
multiplied them by the good nights
I would never divide her smile
her smiles were infinite
how can infinity not equate to forever's
respect is a pride thing and pride can't fit
when love is all you got
all you have left to give
I respect the wind for the reminder
sometimes there are no storms
just gale force winds, just breezes we bask in
just air rustling the branches of trees
I feel the shattering of my bones
they must endure this leaving
it's the reason I believe in ghost
sometimes ghost can reappear
can remember where home was
home is - can recall love
when love was and is
all you will ever have to give

\#

only pieces remain
fragments of promises still intact
we were building forever
at least that was the plan
maybe the blueprints were missing
could have been the steel beams of love
were not strong enough
to bridge more than one tomorrow
more than one I love you at a time
I remember the day
we checked the foundation
mapped out the windows
decided how many doors
forever should have
none of them were exits
they were supposed to be
entrances from everywhere
from anywhere to let more love in
the sky would be the roof
we agreed the clouds and sun
are both the same beautiful
the living room was a garden
we would plant two of every flower
we thought joy was a blossom
thought hope bloomed year round
only requiring us to speak life
to laugh in their presence to grow
I didn't think the chalked outline

what if there were no titles

in the foyer mirrored a body
never viewed a soul up close
it had the form of love
if love ever took shapes
you look like love to me
you look like forever
in human form
reminded me of all the things
my grandmother taught me
she said forever's
are not built in a day
sometimes forever's
begin at a glance
in a walk to nowhere
in a smile ever glowing
your smile seems to travel galaxy's
from wherever you are
to anywhere I am
I guess no one should want
forever in an instant
we know all too well even tomorrows
take time to get here
my grandmother taught me
to love and let
nothing else worth wanting
or having is up to me
I am still working on the letting grandma
may need a little help from heaven
to get out of my own way

\#

the first time
I listened to an audio book
I couldn't tell the difference
between utter amazement and shock
both appeared at the same time
as though they were beckoned
as if I called them by name
I wasn't used to
not holding in my hands
the finished product
of some author's work
bound for perfection
hoping to be caressed
if they had feelings I am sure
books would be jealous
of the advancement
I know the audio wasn't completed
in one take or two the process
is one of preciseness
must have been tedious
I have often wondered
why we have breath
if not to share messages and songs
imagine humans had breath and no mouth
what good would it be
we are constantly replacing purpose
with technology books with audio books
phone calls with text messages

what if there were no titles

actual visits with facetime / skype

books would have to be jealous

how much of the story do we miss

by having it read to us

mother goose style

the hands on approach will soon

be referred to as archaic

a back in the day concept

no one will remember doing it themselves

we are so far ahead of our time

I am beginning to believe

we are traveling backwards

soon the question will be

what good is breath

did you seal your lips accidentally

mistaking glue for lipstick

every human interaction

is being substituted

by an app, program or website

time will someday fight back

instead of using its hands to go around

it may grow angry arms and start

choking sense back into

our seldom used heads

I know time has to notice our misuse of it

gaming and facebooking for hours

watching videos of no consequence

what good is breath

if not used to pass blessings

#

watching someone else walk
does nothing for your legs
exercise videos are only good
if you are moving along
I have watched my path
change directions so many times
still clutching the same dreams
I've been dragging in barrels
most of these seconds since breath
dreams are lighter than you think
and much heavier than they look
I wish I had extra hands to help carry yours
this body was the perfect plan
two hands and two legs per person
just enough to drag dreams
practice will never make you perfect
it will only make you better
at whatever you choose to practice
we keep forgetting
one of the most important lessons
airplanes try and teach us
place on your breathing apparatus
before aiding someone else
I thank God for these ins and outs
for the mountains that fall in my way
for friends with quicker steps than mine
I watch them scatter
at the first glimpse of lightning

what if there were no titles

didn't know

I was born

a lightning rod

I call lightning

some mornings

just to help me write

I got thunder on speed dial

pens are afraid of my right hand

so I carry them by the dozens

you never know when a pen

will friend you

grow feet and scatter

I believe in words

I believe our hearts

carry more instruments

than the biggest

orchestra's and bands

I believe I can

wrap you in enough

chest music you would stay

watch me write songs on paper

that will leave you fully clothed

and completely naked

I got sentences to help you

grow your dreams

I got dreams of you

naked but fully clothed

dragging your dreams

in barrels beside me

\#

there is a thin line

between falling and fallen

sometimes you will never know

exactly when you fell

or even be aware

you are down

you may only remember

the dusting off

not the getting up

sometimes love

will scrape your knees

scuff your elbows

you can't fit real love

and ego's in the same heart

some days love will be

much bigger than you imagined

and there will be days

love may need

your help to walk

love never fails

although we lay claim

it does on the regular

I believe in love

but sometimes

you have to be quiet

patient and let love be love

it may not need or require

your help at all

#

love is never love
when you sit waiting
expecting love to be love
love has the most worst
has the baddest timing
of anything
we associate time with
love shows up
always unexpectedly
always filled with hope
and wonderment
love is more nitro filled balloon
than its celebratory smile
would lead you to believe
love is more race car than bicycle
love is a fireplace
in the Texas summer
at full blaze
piled high with new wood
love is the poem
I keep trying to write
but the words won't stay
where I put them
yea
that's love
yea
that's love
for sure

#

we will often
make the mistake
of thinking faith is a word
faith is more distance
than sound
cannot be measured
in miles
is more space run
than earth walk
imagine drawing a map
you are here
with faith your map
would read
you are there
not that you are not you
with faith you are more
than just you
you are them
everyone
all who believed in you
before you believed in you
those who knew
you were capable
knew you had it in you
have faith in yourself
and be great
for there is greatness
in you

what if there were no titles

#

I feel you are always one breath away

one bidding to the heavens from being mine

I wrote of you in crayon while I was just a boy

unable to dream but I remember vividly

how blue the blue was

how pink was the fragrance of love

tulips were red I knew nothing of roses

how warm the orange glowed

how the black felt chocolate

looked caramel as if I were painting your skin

I would often color in black as if the night

would welcome the union of our sounds

new dreams would think our bodies were music

the neighbors would think we were a band

lying in a bed of instruments

I drew you in stick figures

didn't have a clue

a body could be sculptured

in such grand fashion

I grew tired of explaining

how breathtakingly beautiful

you were in one dimensional drawings

although impossible to see

through the eyes of a boy

I recall every wish long ago before I knew

you would fit my arms perfectly

before my body could agree

I would want you

each occurrence I would stutter

expounding how magnificently

you mirrored the dreams

formed by the mind

of the boy in me

I wonder is it too soon to say

or how much time must one wait

to thank heaven for blessings

to believe heaven has blessed him

I want to send heaven flowers

tell the angels to stop watching you

they look at you as I do

as if they want you too

when is too soon to say

I wished for you

or how many days should I fast

before I taste you like dinner

there has to be a schedule

heaven keeps watch of

keeps time in, I would mark you down as taken

replace your photo with the stick figures

I still remember how to draw

how much time is too soon - how many days is too long

why did heaven forge you so divinely intricate

so unapologetically stunning

I will ask when they reply the boy in me waits

completely aware you stand

only one breath away

one half wish and a dream from here

#

I thought of you
convinced my mind
to cease
told myself to stop
demanded I quit
made a sacred vow
I even pinkie sweared
crossed my fingers twice
and suddenly out of nowhere
I thought of you
often I make the mistake
of thinking your eyes are prayers
thinking you are a goddess
thinking you are supposed to be here
I know you don't know
how you cross my mind
sideways and backwards
replay your arrival daily
afraid to watch you leave
scared you won't return
recalling that laugh
a quarter note from glory
somewhere in your walk
I heard the choir sing
I thought of you
after the rain left
before the water fell
between the rain drops

on the upstrike of thunder

on the down flash of lightning

I thought of you

keep demanding I quit

every time I forget

bit my lip to blood

hoping my mouth

would stop this chanting

this calling out your name

I thought of you

when I turned the lights off

the moment I turned them back on

before I went to sleep

in the toss and the turn of waking

before the monsters came

after the dreams were gone

I thought of you

while listening

to the breeze

as the grass bowed

in reverence

with the song

of morning birds

I thought of you

I must conclude

thinking of you

is the only way

I know how to say

Amen

what if there were no titles

#

never think

I stopped here

not on purpose

there are plans

in my feet

I am not aware of

move feet move

some mission are mysteries

some mysteries are missions

some days last longer than others

some nights are better than days

I rose chasing the thought of you

felt you near me while I slept

maybe your subconscious

wants you to be here

could be we met before

in a dream

if I close my eyes

tight enough

I can hear you breathing

purpose is a mountain

we can only climb together

I've been journeying

on my own far too long

not to notice

these feet

need someone

to walk with

I only see you

in wishful thinking

in closed eye

slumber sessions

with destiny

I stopped here

on purpose

to let you know

purpose asked me

to bring you along

the very next time

we tread mountains

jump trials

the very next time

we search for love

in the valleys of life

near the foothills

of forever

these feet need you

to accompany them

purpose

asked me

who you

were

to me

I told her

you were

her

replacement

\#

love is the

quintessential

ingredients

for dreams to grow

to become whole

sky walking is tricky

clouds move too much

to know where

your next step will be

can't predetermine

your destination

when new is not just a word

but the destination

you are riding air to arrive

love is everything and more

it holds the greatest benefit

and the over powering

detriment to our existence

I love love

so you can forget

thinking I don't love you

I love you simply because

this journey demands

I love completely

negating the fact

or possibility it may never

find its way

back home

#

I
didn't leave
would never
run away
fathers have
missions
not of their
choosing
if they have
seeds
the choice
was made
for them
when they
created
seedlings
love
could never
leave
it doesn't have
legs to go
I left love you's
at the door
of your heart
hoping
they could
call you
home

what if there were no titles

#

art and artist somehow believe
the art created carries them
your creations are extensions of you
it is you who carry your creations
whether book, canvas or song
I have grown accustomed to wondering
where they come from
these conjuring's, messages
no one can hear but I
truthfully I don't actually hear them
it is an unexplainable process
but hear is what I know
or is it here is what I know
everything we do is out of love
there is no such thing as hate
if we believe love conquers all
how could hate win or withstand
the power of hearts
although the heart
is not the place our love resides
I can't explain but we've been taught
things we take for granted
there are lessons we accept
were given us in good faith
told to us as truth's
seldom searching for truth
how can anyone build truth
from things they don't know

I don't know how to tell you

we don't know

the things we know

or thought in our chest we knew

our words will sound garbled

the garbage we cherish

the shiny things we give importance

what is important

are the things we can't explain

the ones we take for granted

histories of traditions

has worn us weary

stolen our fight

we wear knowledge as truth

on foundations of smoke

looking good from a distance

but smoke is just smoke

all I'm trying to tell you

is know yourself

the same lesson stolen from the pyramids

gifted to continents to fool us of its origin

know thyself

is love - creates faith

in people who don't believe in faith

and is the only truth we will ever know

the truth to be - true

know thyself

then you will know everything

you will ever need to know

what if there were no titles

#

we often build on our own
more purpose blocking obstacles
with our imagination
than those actually
standing in our path
it is the human condition
conditioning us to believe
we are not properly equipped
to carry these burdens
these prizes we hold in our grasp
the greatness in us suppressed
by the doubt we've discovered
over time, told over and over
we could not, will not
could never be
who we say or what we say
our sound not as clear
our words shaky
believing in ourselves
is the only thing we have
to combat unbelievers
we must find our balance
there will be days you are awake
walking about still dazed
it will take you to wake you
from your walking sleep
you can easily Linus yourself
carry a cloud of inactivity

above your head

thinking you can't

truth is you won't

you refuse to give that all

you speak of - that everything

you reference so often

shared with others

you will not be aware

you have become

self-surface satisfied

believing the majesty

of your own existence

you are supposed to believe in you

but only when you are moving

in a realm of believability

doing nothing

is simply doing nothing

be great

but do great things

find greatness

in the use of your gifts

we are gods

not the humans

we profess

in the wailing

and complaining

and all the other

sounds we make

Note to self: reread until it sinks in

what if there were no titles

\#

I've been banging my head
against wishes
against ideas and thoughts
trying to understand why
why love lost the forever properties
of years we cherish - those we celebrate
of our grandparents and watch in movies
love used to be love
it was worth mentioning
in places now banning it's presence
vows snapped as twigs
we don't even love love
happy signatures written in ink
on court documents easily erased
I think it goes back
some yesterdays from here
we stopped playing outside
it was in a game of hopscotch
jacks has been removed from shelves
double-dutch was a builder of confidence
there was so much trust discovered in a seesaw
we found truth in the daily 40 yard sprint
learning our feet are not as fast
as we say they are
but there was still the promise of tomorrow
we participated in daily olympics
of youth of being young
an argument meant you disagreed

but only disagreed
a fight was just a fight
tomorrow we would start new
we have forgotten how to start new
how to begin from here
and not over
I think it was outside we learned
life was the daily wins and losses
accumulated - had no reflection
on a tomorrow safely hidden
until it arrives - until we discover
ourselves jovially, joyfully
basking in the rays of its sun
with the same people we call friends
just out of repetition of meeting here
the air around us for comfort
the sound of happy filled our ears
and now wonder why
love isn't love anymore - I will tell you
run a 40 yard sprint to test your feet
play a game of double-dutch
see if your coordination remains intact
for love is a seesaw - no one is always on top
and no one is always on the bottom
arguments were just arguments, every day we knew
love was olympic trials we passed and failed
came again tomorrow to try again
we knew then in winning and losing
life at its best is only in the try again

\#

there is a lesson
in creating
and of creation
people will love you
for the things
you create for them
and despise you
for the things
you create for you
there will always be
those who know
you better than
you know you
and know what
is best for you
do not worry
those are the rules
this life comes with
unspoken procedures
often finding wind
enough to speak
just keep creating
keep following
your purpose
it is not one lane
or a one way street
purpose is a highway
with twisting and turning

over paths

and under ways

each lane is built

for four way traffic

you can get run over

if you don't keep moving

standing still will become

problematic

if not in motion

dust will gather

on your purpose

we treat the back

of our minds

as though it is equipped

with hands and fingers

grudges are too big to hold

too heavy to carry

on your way to destiny

let it go

you have bigger dreams

requiring all the strength

you possess and more

we have a weigh station

reserved for packages

set aside for the baggage

we carry

for the yesterday's

still in our possession

let them go

#

every day there are lessons

in moments, in days

we considered not ours

so we let them leave - gave them their free

time is a class we are

automatically attending

being alive is the only

requirement for signing up

there is power in the struggle

whether we win or lose

no one taught us to keep score

this earth is too large of a playing field

there is strength in knowing

muscles gained from lifting

things imagined and conjured

out of thin air we gave substance

there is strength in discovering

in finding you must learn

you have to study to know

there is unbelievable knowledge

in listening, in closed mouth

open ears - hold your tongue quiet

do not mistake being grown

for not being able to grow

every minute we are growing

one way or the other we are still growing

you will continue this process

until rest meets you - until breath cease to visit

#

if in the

beginning

was the word

that would

also mean

babies

are speaking

the language

of the beginning

just because

we think

they are just sounds

doesn't mean

they are just sounds

they lay prostrate

as David

when he prayed

sometimes

crawl about

wearing their knees

in daily conversations

with the most high

in constant prayer

it should

make you wonder

what babies

are telling

heaven about us

#

why is it we always display
the simple side of ourselves
knowing mere days from now
we will be completely complicated
there has to be a methodology
to the strategic placement
of our smiles - just yesterday
you were all smiles
I guess I must've worn
out their welcome
I remember how joy sounds
how there was a melody
in your eyes
in the movement
of your lips
it seems as though
the corners of your mouth
stay in rest
sick or bed ridden
turned down for sleep
simplicity is never
the best introduction
when we are opera
a two person concerto
it gets too hard
to play all the instruments
to perfection
when you didn't know

the melody would change
didn't know
the oboe and flute had solo's
you played my heart
to a violin's perfection
I once loved the violin
there is a simple side to loving
song as clear as the alto sax
I keep forgetting how
I can't remember when
these notes I've been keeping
are not written in my handwriting
I can't make out the markings
the scribblings of promises
made when things were simple
loving is simply complicated
we went from a two-step
to a fox trot with no lessons
on how to stay in rhythm
often I find myself out of step
I am back to practicing walking
one foot at a time
it's hard to dance alone
when for years you learned
the rhythm of another's heartbeat
was the perfect melody to help you
move your feet - loving used to be simple
now even smiling
has become so complicated

\#

I always carry two dimes
two quarters, two nickels
and four pennies in my pocket
I've found no matter
what I decide to purchase
I have the exact amount
the practice of getting better
starts by refining the simplest
processes at the start of our day
I have a smile laying rest
on the pillow beside my head
it greets me at first eye opening
not saying there are bad nights
even if the one before this sun
was one of the worst
my morning smile is there
come sunshine or tears
with a smile on your face
your eyes will view the new day
as one of the greatest events in history
this one came alone
with no help
it arrived promiseless
not a one of these new days
were accompanied by attachments
or the slightest piece of promise
not one fraction of difference
than the ones preceding it

we are hands on

life designers

for hands off

gives away our ability

to mold, to form

to build better out of worse

to carve excellence into

every flaw we find

there is always flaws

cracks in our armor

a missing firing pen

in our tongues

some days one of our

running shoes will be absent

there will be times you feel absent

feel as if you left you somewhere

some days it will take tears

to get your legs to move

pain will be your closest confidant

the miracle of sense is to always have

the exact amount - it is in the preciseness

of change... the rustling of coins

we will often find pleasure

in the simplest events

joy in a returned smile

confidence in knowing

just yesterday you didn't know

if you would make it this far

and amazingly you are here

what if there were no titles

\#

I must believe

I dreamed you here

I dream the same dream

every night it's the same

it begins dark sky - black

no moon for guidance

covered in an array of stars

brilliant and colorful

so much closer than usual

I may have touched a few

on purpose

may have tried to hold them

longer than humanly allowed

my grandmother's warned me

told me such a thing was possible

I had forgotten their words

until the darkness formed

they both said one day

I would close my eyes in need

and wake up in glory

sometimes I think you are a miracle

a manifestation of hope

I stopped wishing

the day you arrived

didn't think you would stay

but made arrangements

planned for forever's

with no idea how long

a forever should be

or should last

I have to believe

I dreamed you here

my imagination

could never be good enough

heaven had to lend

more than one hand

in the process

I have discovered

how it feels when your voice

misses time in my ear

didn't know a day

could last an eternity

I had to have dreamed you here

had to have begged or prayed

in my lonely for this blessing

you are a blessing

a body filled of wishes

a manifestation of hope

I didn't know hope

was so beautiful when it walks

so melodic when it speaks

I told my dreams

they were no longer needed

she is here already

thanked my grandmother's

for the warning

and pray I get this right

what if there were no titles

#

I used to catch Praying Mantids
sit and watch them for hours
never once saw them pray
over time I discovered most of the things
I was told as matters of fact weren't facts
were not truly matters at all
were not to be taken literal
there has to be an adjustment
a period of recanting to justify
why nothing was what it was
nothing meant what I thought
even left in the same sentences
I don't know why these thoughts
arrived today as if they were beckoned
as if conscious has a voice of its own
I practiced reading between the lines
steadied my fingers to follow the words
read dictionaries so I would be ready
when you approached snail fast
I waited
to greet your sound
your words were anvil light
felt real to the touch
first time I saw prayers
the first time things mattered
at least for a while
until
until I was awakened to find

nothing was what I thought
or what you said it was
until nothing mattered at all
not even the sound you gifted
and took back
changed your tone
I am not for sure why
you use your outside voice
inside so frequently
why your eyes fail to see sun
why you treasure anger in mornings
wrestle with hush at night
I didn't know sadness until you
formally introduced us
we've become close
almost the best of friends
I once believed sound
was the most precious commodity
we humans possessed
didn't know tongues could sideways
twist lies into gems
make crooked almost straight
truth as elusive as a bear
wearing the wings of a humming bird
I valued the giving
there is honor in gifts
even if the gifts are taken back
before ever revealing
its true contents

what if there were no titles

#

trying to recall my first smile is impossible
attempting to remember my first heartbreak
isn't easy to locate the overwhelming feeling
of left still fresh... it doesn't matter who left
I will always question how good is good?
your favorite cake or pie creates a marginal line
this is how we define good in the beginning
eventually we will discover what we think we like
but how good is good?
how does great taste?
the questions will keep coming
we keep tossing answers until one sticks
until the answer fits so well in our mouth
it becomes the voice of our heart
our heart has a voice you know
in the beginning we accept pieces of love
mere fragments of hearts
before we find how all feels
all will forever be the prime suspect
in the case for hearts
in the foundation of forever's
until we know how good is good?
how great is great? - is love a place?, or a person?
does forever exist? if so
how do we get there from here?
I need to know how good is good?
place it side by side with my best
my best should be so much better

than good - so much bigger than all
it has to be built of destiny
I need to know how good is good?
this good will be the measuring tool
I use as justification for beginnings
for always, for tomorrows
for this next
I feel quickly approaching
how good should good be?
should it be laced with all or fear?
we discovered fear in the first left
leaving has a tendency to never be gone
to remain as shadows
long after space and time
vacated the premises
have stolen our good
but how good is good?
how do we make it better?
where do we find this best?
others constantly search for
there can be no great or best
if we don't know how good is good?
or how all feels when it touches you
I know how all feels when it brushes
against my smile - when it holds my hand
when it touches my good and forms best
from here I just need to know if you know?
or ever thought you would need to answer
how good is good?

#

I had hoped my life would explain my love
and my words would be the love I live
somewhere I forgot literacy is a gift
some would rather give back than keep
not all who reads accepts what is written
I discovered how to hide me in rhymes
I stopped rhyming some time ago
but kept writing thinking no one noticed
or no one said they noticed
pages were my sanctuary
until your ears became available
I am not used to listeners
actually listening
we played sound verses sound
not listening to listen
you became sanctuary
not that I would hide myself there
but I could give you me
and not fear the giving
not be frightened of consequences
I trusted you with me and can't remember
the last time I trusted me with me
we consider so many acts making love
to me love is an ear for a sanctuary
a smile to keep frowns from bursting through
making love to me is listening
I guess you sound of love to me
you listen as though you could love me too

you look like joy to me
and I the jovial one
had never witnessed joy
I've drawn joy before
sketched it from memory
I know how joy feels
when it rest in my chest
your words are pillows
resting in my chest
I would invite you in
if you had not already
found residence
I welcome the sound of you
the smile you bring
I will proudly share
your pain and joy
you are here, sanctuary
discovered my need
for solitude, for comfort
didn't know these were needs
never knew I would want you
opened heart welcome mat you
to come sit with me
not even I knew I was lonely
I don't want to need you
but can't imagine not needing you
I grow in gratitude - in grateful
for you - wishing you knew
you are sanctuary

what if there were no titles

#

I've been building promises of hope

the hope of my grandfather's absence

hope of my grandmother's America

of my mother's love and faith

hope of my father's free

I've been building promises out of faith

faith somehow I can father as God meant

I can love as Allah meant

I can be this God in me

sometimes hope is hard to mold

to forge into promises

we have promises to keep that are centuries old

left by those with no voice to voice theirs

I find myself building promises

out of broken promises

there are those I broke myself and many

others forgot they made are still here

promises never leave - can't be discarded

I am building promises out of prayers

these knees must be older than I am

the way the earth accepts them from memory

all promises are made of great intentions

but great intentions can't make promises

I've been building promises out of footsteps

I keep walking this road where none appears

told me the one less traveled would be the one

I've been building promises out of love

I thought love was the foundation

pillars of all we are

sometimes love can't make promises

can't hold them in this fragile heart

or in hands carrying too many burdens

to distinguish the difference

I've been building promises out of tears

I have held enough of them

to know their texture

to know the origin and why they fall

from promises undressed and ruptured

I have been building promises out of words

pieces of me I bleed on remanufactured trees

there may be something here to last

can't take me back once it's given

can't unlove once you've been loved

once you've been written into scriptures

I will write you in verses

as the prophets of old

I am unable to build promises out of sound

lips are not good foundations

or sturdy enough to construct promises

I keep building promises

out of everything I am - knowing the only way

they could ever last... if you help to build

these same promises out of everything you are

lasting promise are those promises

which care not why they are created

care not from whence they came

it only matters they have been made

what if there were no titles

\#

I didn't know these bones
considered the skin protecting them
to be armor - fastened securely
over every inch of this frame
if that were the case
I should have been prepared
when these cracks appeared
when you battle ready creeped
past my defenses, climbed under my skin
hid quietly undiscovered
if I would have known these bones
were brittle - couldn't withstand your smile
weren't tested for stability
would bend at the thought of you
would nearly break themselves if you left
I would have practiced safety first
would have purchased a shield or chest plate
this heart wasn't cleared for departure
hadn't been dusted for years
there were stains from the last invasion
I didn't see the cracks until
your good morning awakened the sun
in my life - I could watch the beams
kaleidoscope my secret places
openly display some parts were missing
this skin should lose its job
it didn't perform as the instructions permitted
I should have layered the whole of it

with eyes enough to see your approach
there is no mention of how you got here
past the armor I depended on all this time
I believed it was better equipped for service
don't know when these cracks appeared
can't tell if your beauty is a weapon
this skin welcomed you unannounced
asked you to live here - all of this is new
these cracks - your smile - your suitcases
unpacked cluttering my chest
should have bought a chest plate
wish this skin would have warned me
I would have hired a cleaning service
skeletons are hard to drag away
most of them mine I kept hidden
until your sun revealed they no longer fit
can't be of service - should have been tossed
after the last invasion
don't know when these cracks broke through
when the armor failed, when my defenses shut down
or the exact day this skin should've lost its job
didn't know I wasn't whole until your sound
caressed my soul the tenderness explained
those missing parts don't matter
keep the skin everything is worth saving
I could never be whole without you
I was practicing whole while waiting
the skin knew and made the cracks appear
how else would the suit cases fit

what if there were no titles

\#

my parents didn't tell tall tales

of starks delivering babies

or ghost in closets

but love

I wish had been hi ho silver

or dudley do right explained

if they spoke of all the things broken

in order to fix what remains

or how your insides can be torn apart

the best of you hidden in memories

of skin sensitive to sun

I would tell my sons

if ever they ask

where does love come from?

I would tie their hands

behind their backs

twist the strings together

tightly in their shoes

tie a bandana loosely

around their eyes

place tape over their lips

sit quietly for at least an hour

untie them

loosen their laces

remove the tape from their mouths

tell them love comes from heaven

you will never see it coming

I am unable to offer enough words

to properly prepare you
for loves arrival
you will feel absent from yourself
lost - incapable of finding your way
you will feel bound
ropeless
can't move sometimes
speechless
your words will abandon you
it will be the first time you know free
fear will reside in the core of your being
you will be afraid love will leave
you will never be ready
her smile will become the sole reason
you believe breath is still here
I am powerless to protect you
you will never be ready
just remember
when love comes
bid her entrance
treat her to the best you
you've been taught to be
if she ever chooses to leave
let her
bid her farewell
and safe passage
prepare for the dark
you will never be ready
when love comes

#

some days the pain in your heart
makes your fingers sticky
you will struggle to hold on
to everything you touch
the darkest day you can recall
is the day love let go
you will wish for glue
you will pray your hands are a vise
ask God for more strength in fingers
it is easy to forget
love comes and goes on its own
you can never hold it in your palms
it stays because it wants to
it leaves because it has to
there are classes in leaving
we didn't know existed
until gone arrived all lonely
and hushed – mouth full of quiet
I learned silence from clouds
some days the sun
will make them leave
will rush them to move
you have to listen fast
takes notes of their gentle passing
have you ever prayed arthritis
would lock your hands closed
didn't care about the pain
just wanted to know

how keep felt

how much holding is holding on

how does stay look close up

I find myself saying the strangest things

somewhere in my mind

is a unforgettable memory

of the aromatic flavor of kisses

my lips are sensitive that way

they traced every cell of her mouth

remembered how the corners

possessed no downward motion

how her eyes welcomed good mornings

how lilac sweet good nights sounded in quiet

some days I wish my fingers were magnets

and love retained metallic properties

wish my eyes could project images

I wish days were a book

had chapter titles

I could turn the pages

could search the table of contents

some days I ask God for a reset button

place it on the edge of this heart

that breaks so easily

cracks at the sound

of this voice in my head

sometimes I wish away my hands

cry away these memories

I don't know why

will never know why

what if there were no titles

can't understand why
lonely is a village
a bed with no pillows
an uncomfortable sleeping arrangement
with lonesome
I've learned to sleep comfortable
when keeping is not kept when gone is the plan
when leaving is only the method of catching up
when you catch them looking for themselves
in the bathroom mirror
catch them practicing
a so long or a good bye in a whisper
love comes and goes on its own
you can never hold it in your palms
it stays because it wants to
it leaves because it has to
we beg it to stay even after we've learned
heaven made other arrangements
for this heart that breaks so easily
creating space to gather new memories
negating the fact I have grown
very fond of the ones I presently possess
we all have an affinity for the usual
a quaint affection for the common
we've developed or come accustomed to
God… if only right here
on the edge of my memories
on the soft portion of my temple
there was a reset button

\#

we've built continents
and nations out of traditions
and religious documents
but have yet to discover
how to love
how to cherish
and display compassion
we pray to deities
saints and gods
for instructions
sit patiently in silence
waiting for answers
that may never come
some nights I lay
eyes closed, hands clasp
candles for light, a shimmering of calm
flickering across ceiling and walls
tears falling, chanting the same words
I have heard others use in honor
pay homage to my ancestors
for the journey
for the pain of centuries
to my parents for the gift
life is a blessing
I meditate to clear my chakra's
burn sage to cleanse the room
of bad thoughts and spirits
in all the years I never envisioned

what if there were no titles

religion is a woman - a goddess

I pray I get this right

there is a sacred dance of hands

I'd like to share with you

you are the majestic melody

I would bow to

kneel at your altar

we will call this

our worship service

it will begin as I wash your feet

your hair

rinse away memories

of all who wasn't me

treat your body as the altar it is

I will anoint it with oils

watch your cup runneth over

I have learned the mercy of fingers

you are deserving

of these ancient secrets

this is

our worship service

I know how to speak to heaven

In Kemet I read

it rest between your thighs

my tongue will draw the symbols

from the halls of pyramids

on the walls of every sacred place

you weren't aware

was sacred and holy

this is
our worship service
have you ever had someone
kneel at your altar
until you showered uncontrollably
I studied for years
the sacred dance of hands
just to share the dance with you
this is
our worship service
I never envisioned
religion was a woman
a goddess to the utmost
I will treat your altar
with the ceremonious care
of my ancestors
consecrated by the heavens
loving has always been sacred
these are the secrets
of my father's father
and generations and generations
before him
hidden in the tomb of kings
for a millennia
only resurrected for this moment
the sacred of sacred
the holy of holies
this is
our worship service

what if there were no titles

\#

I try so hard

to remember

and forget

to cherish

and let free

these recent storms

have taught me

a most valuable lesson

love is a lightning strike

a quick flash of brilliance

you must be

open eyes to see

open chest to feel

and open mind

to understand

when you love

don't love as oceans

although edgeless

love as space

as galaxies

love will present you

with more you to discover

more happy than smiles

more reach

than arms allow

true love

will forever be

limitless

\#

most are unaware

storms are used

to wash away

to remove things

we didn't know

needed to be removed

I've been in love with rain

since the first pair of shoes

my parents bought for me

found joy in puddles

if you wonder why boys

like to play in mud

it is because they know

soon the rains will come

and cleanse the dirt

there are no reasons for joy

to rest securely in pain

or why tears become

the best water

to wash my face with

I've discovered comfort

in the lonely love left me

as a companion

I used to worry about tomorrows

now I make the most of every today

if I could choose who to love

I would draw a diagram

with arrows and footnotes

what if there were no titles

that is exactly why hearts

don't have eyes or ears

hearts don't know listen

and never met stop

my heart doesn't know

what you look like

can't hear the description

I try so hard to write

the perfect words to

I have learned to value

seconds more than minutes

smiles more than sounds

I am learning

the lessons of hearts

no eyes to see

can't hear your words

but I will know you inside out

for my heart

doesn't know listen

never met stop

so I guess this is a one way trip

a solemn destination

to see if hearts can speak

a language of their own

I still find joy and puddles

and adore how the rain

washes away those things

I didn't know needed

to be washed away

\#

I would have to believe
we use more than
ten percent of our brain
when emotions
becomes attached
to our mind and heart
simultaneously
there are examples
of feelings
being experienced
miles away
some thoughts
are shared
the instant
one mind locates
their whereabouts
I believe my heart
could find you
if you wish for me
if we want
at the same time
our spirits
will search our wants
our souls will meet
I sometimes find you
sitting in my dreams
uninvited
but truly welcomed

what if there were no titles

#

just because my jacket
was laced tightly from the back
doesn't mean I deserved it
they didn't understand why
why my house was filled
with broken pencils
why I felt the need to slice pens in half
ink everywhere, some stains remain whole
there were puddles of black and blue
some rooms resembled finger painting of sorts
the walls no longer bare
alphabets everywhere
some words had to be drug into existence
I know how sentences are formed
how tragic it can be to make sense
of the senseless
to make good out of bad
sometimes you are required
to build from scratch
some days they will reveal to you
how they want to be mentioned
I once enjoyed the fresh start of thoughts
now I know fresh starts are not fresh
they came out of need
out of necessary
penability cannot but realized
from holding pens
you discover the intrinsic

medicinal powers of writing

in the moving of pens

in the patient carvings on pages

most will not understand the process

you will wear a jacket

laced tightly from the back

they will consider you mad

will want to cut off

one of your ears

the king will have your tongue removed

the report will have you reclassified

you won't be human, or man or woman

they will write you imbalanced

will prescribe numbing prescriptions

they will want to silence the voices

you've been aware of since you

arrived from heaven years ago

artist are only loved

when they can art no more

they will gather your etchings

your creations

will call you a magnificent thinker

you will be labeled genius

will bind you in text books

just as they did with the jacket

securely laced and tied from the back

lie about how you formed thoughts

out of the goodness of your heart

not how you were going crazy

what if there were no titles

to get them out of your head
they won't know you begged
for clemency, to be free of pens
you prayed for the safety of trees
picketed and sacrificed for rain forest
these words are not martyr's
they didn't crucify themselves
you made them out of sound
gave them volume on heavens instructions
and no one will ever understand why
why my house was filled with broken pencils
why I felt the need to slice pens in half
why ink was everywhere
my tongue stained black and blue
sometimes red - when I wrote in blood
call me crazy it's ok - write of me
however you see fit
but know this is God's work
these are heavens hands
I must do what must be done
to remove and silence these voices
these echoes - in my head
I knew this would be my duty
when they separated me
from my mother's womb
this is God's work - these hands
are heavens hands
none of this is of me
this be God's work - not mine

#

we often associate cuts
surgeries, stitches and heartache
in the same category
we call everything pain
pain is relative
I have shadowed me for months
wanting to know where I go
sitting in the same spot
replaying the same day
over and over as though
I got lost in a moment
left my conscious unconscious
maybe wishing I could locate
the you of yesterday
wondering through my present
pain is relative - distant cousin
or sibling from the other side
all I know is we are together
reunioning, often sharing
a single celebration
a Merry Tuesday
or some unmentioned holiday
we've made a tradition of
it is easy to get got
if you pay more attention
to where you've been
than where you think
you're going

what if there were no titles

you will never make it

the past is beautiful

scenic and majestic

it will matter

how you tell yourself

you were in it

I once constructed

another me

not to walk through

my now days

but to live in my thens

I made me better - different

I can't be the only one

who redecorates my yesterday's

painting a more coloristic background

changed the back drop

wore a nicer tie

reworded conversations

I know we should have had

but didn't

we call everything pain

it sounds so much better that way

no one would listen

if we told the story

and we hurt ourselves

open hands no fingers pointing

we love to point fingers

we grew up thinking

that's what they are for

blame being the one
innocence the three aiming back
we were taught
and skillfully learned
to pay no never mind
pain and I, me and pain
or pain and me has been
too many places together
spent too much time sitting
in the same spot
trying to force a yesterday
to be better
to make this now
easy to swallow
I don't call pain anymore
and don't answer
when he shows up unannounced
I don't make eye contact with him
when passing him in my yesterday's
I never tell him of my tomorrow's
I know he wants to hang
we are family
and have visited many places
now I just want to be alone
with my thoughts
see everything
as it is and was
black, white and grey
or no color at all

#

yesterday I discovered

pieces of last year

hiding in the unmade bed

underneath my pillow

some of my days past

are recirculating

frequently now

missed too many her's

for she to still have

any semblance of residence

in the sound of lost echoes

thoughts are flowing faster

gusting stronger than ever

if should had rules

a new ballot has to be created

to write new laws

during the next election

I thought she

was an always

or a lasting forever

didn't take her for a never

she was the battle in the war

molded my soul of white flags

in the very beginning

got me picking stars

that haven't shot yet

wishing love

had a steering wheel

or a nice set of brakes

can't withstand the gravity

or rather the g-force of taking

her sharpened curves

too quickly

every decision

an unwilling

unstable molotov cocktail

with only two choices

either we were blowing up

or burning down

neither

has the rhythm

of tomorrow

if ever I am asked

what happened

it will go unanswered

I will leave the bed unmade

glue the pillows securely

to the fitted sheets

and sleep on the floor

to practice picking myself up

recovery will always be

an I thing

leave the past in the past

get some now

if not

how will I ever

be ready for tomorrow

what if there were no titles

\#

I must have been about eleven
one day at the local swimming pool
my brother tossed me in the deep
said the best way to learn to swim
is to have to save yourself
in St Croix, Virgin Islands
islanders and ocean are friends
I the Texan am cousin to lakes
while on a small row boat
in the dark of night - moonless
I was so afraid of the boat capsizing
felt I had forgotten how to swim
we were going out for nets
they placed them in places
on god knows where
the plan was to retrieve
the contents to complete
the cookout on the beach
I kept asking
which way to shore
there was a fire blazing bright
once a source of warmth
bottles of rum
and uncut coconuts
lay waiting for our return
none of which
were anywhere in sight
this rocking got me thinking

how small waves
in lakes were nothing
not even kin
to waves in oceans
how swimming
could be easily forgotten
especially if per chance
I choose the wrong direction
in which to go
the nets were heavy
forced us to rock
even more
they were full
of everything
full of things
I had only seen
in pictures
in movies
or documentaries
Jock Cousteau
would be proud
fear is unsettling
when men can't speak it
can't fathom how
a yard or a mile
could mean death
the wrong direction
would mean lost
maybe lost forever

what if there were no titles

#

in the beginning was the word
I believe that's why
my mother read to me
books written by Dr. Seuss
he created everything from thought
I wasn't aware of it then
but the mind holds all things
at the ready
you can't get ready
if you are not already in motion
moving towards better
searching for the more in you
she told me to read Peter
study to show thyself
taught me of Ezekiel
David and Solomon
of trials by Jacob and Job
presented examples
of withstanding and withstood
told me how feet, purpose and passage
should become the best of friends
how gone ain't gone
it's just not there sometimes
you don't need to recall lessons until the test arrives
you should pray some test never come
I grew a great adoration for the power of words
not that words matter – truth is they do
but sound be a completely different story

I would tell my story

explain how I got this throat full of positive

when negatives shows up

how these hands learn to praise dance

while writing scriptures

how these feet are laced tightly

with motivation for shoes

when all that exist

is dissention, anger and doubt

I can tell how doubt is worse than fear

how fear comes from not knowing

from not believing you were equipped

how this mind holds everything at the ready

but there are chapters still in writing

in progress - I have learned progress

sometimes has a hole in the bottom

doesn't come with instructions

can resemble a dust storm in the desert

a house with no walls

how sometimes progress can go in reverse

when you're not watching

how reverse can be forward and

sometimes moving fast can get you lost

I remember Green Eggs Ham

and Jesus on the mount

how sometimes a little fish and bread

can feed a village or a nation

when written in the proper context

these words sometimes taste of fish and bread

what if there were no titles

I know how pain looks up close
how to help others when you can't help yourself
there are hidden blessings in words
you can discover hiding in your heart
when you dig deep enough - when you know
the Grinch stole more than a fantasy
you may have to run on water
every now and then
when this street ends
when the highway collapses
its left up to you to build a way to keep going
when friends penciled you out
when they say you done lost your mind
when they get mad at you
for what you're going through
my mother taught me that staying
will often be much harder than leaving
and that leaving gives way
to giving up or in – ain't no tangible difference
it ain't no battle for real
when you know the battle is real
when you understand words been here before you
they have withstood and are still standing
my mother read to me so I could learn to read
taught me sound so I could speak to nations
neither she or I knew – Dr. Seuss and Jesus
Enoch and Akbar – Langston and Angelo
Moses and Dr. Ben – Isaiah and my pen
could all taste like fish and bread sometimes

\#

yesterday I learned
of our need for water
along with our fear of the same
we pray for rain then instantly beg it to stop
we are familiar with the displacement power
of hurricanes, of torrential storms
for me water and poetry is the source
the reason I was born and for my existence
I've watched with teary eyes this art
this gift of burdens bundle itself into
the catalyst for falling outs - arguments
the cause of friends forgetting friendships
there was a time poetry was the fireplace
the safe house we gathered to share our pain
we worshiped - these words were our prayers
now we have disagreements over who the best is
there can only be today's best
tomorrow everyone should be better
who is to say getting better is not best anyway
we spew positive sounds through negative lips
gather to teach our youth of love
with anger in our hearts
poetry has always been the truth to me
the way I found the origin of the roots of me
I see it being used to destroy our word community
how can we build better when everybody thinks they know
how can we repair wounds when no one wants to show
this is not how poetry is supposed to grow

what if there were no titles

\#

as a boy I was a collector
I would capture butterflies
caterpillars, bumblebees
marveled at hummingbirds
gazed as eagles soared
out of reach of my imagination
it took time to understand
holding a butterfly too tight
will destroy its beauty
return it to the state
from which it grew
make it again caterpillar
render its wings useless
I learned bumblebees for defense
will suicide itself - sting you
knowing it only has one to offer
a choice of death in lieu of capture
discovered beauty in colorful rocks
how the most lovely of them
can't be found on the surface
you must get your hands dirty
I learned how to love
by watching the sun
no jealousy exist
when clouds day come
when thunder and rain arrives
when darkness blocks its radiance
learned of unconditional from trees

watched as their blossoms were taken
time allows every year their removal
I watched them stand proud and naked
not ashamed of losing as if they know
as if time taught them
only after everything is lost
will their season come again
I've learned love is a season
it can last for minutes or a lifetime
I learned how to love
from watching seasons
knowing change isn't always welcomed
but it's coming - so welcome it
some days it will be too hot
you will not find solace
in the skin you're in
you will require an umbrella sometimes
to keep from being drenched
there will be days a light jacket
will not be enough for survival
a blanket will not suffice for warmth
you will miss the body heat
you thought would be there
through freezing cold
you knew were not to be yours alone
I learned of love from the wind
hurricanes can uproot your comfort
displace your happy
steal all your belongings

what if there were no titles

it took years to accumulate
some days the breeze
will be beautiful
it will gust at times
make you lose your hat
will mess up your hair
you spent so much time beautifying
will rip the important scribblings
you've stored on pages
from your grasp
I learned how to love
from counting tears
although I lost count some time ago
I know love can make you
begin again at one
the boy in me is still
teaching me of love
I am still watching
seasons change
feeling the wind
listening to the storms
gathering lessons
some days I find myself
praying for rain, and sun
and clouds and calm
wishing there was enough
in me to know but knowing
there are lessons needed
I am still learning to love

#

I am leaning
toward the belief
music began before the first instrument
before the first tree was hollowed
to create the first drum
it had to have its start with love or loving
when an embrace in quiet moments
led to hearing the simultaneous beating
locating its echo hidden under skin
listening to the rhythm - not calling it love
but knowing its origin lies in legends
believing it is the original source of magic
the best inventions are fashioned of tragedy
when there is nothing left but silence
when we stand open hand and empty vessel
we attempt to force our minds
to comprehend this melody of life
these tones of emotions so thick with joy
so full of promise, we appreciate the darkness
long before promises could ever be broken
in a time when sound couldn't express
when words had not the power to bend
to break apart leaving thoughts shattered
still they were aware somehow it must be shared
there had to be a period of trial and error
a time when the discovery
wasn't considered discovered yet
imagine a man sitting alone

what if there were no titles

eyes wet with lonesome
using both hands pounding
lightly on his chest to mimic
the sound remembered
I believe man formed drums
out of lonely - out of need
out of necessity to know
wanting to hear a lasting embrace
hoping to share it with the wind
in the right cadence - she
where ever she may be
would hear, would remember
and know it was the sound of them
I am almost certain - close to positive
music was the antidote for a broken heart
long before anyone ever thought
a heart could possibly be broken
before we knew memories
were the river our tears crawl out of
songs were written in honor of yesterdays
in remembrance of glad tidings
without music there would be no songs
without drums - there would be no embrace
no rhythms to dance my lonely to
to beat my chest to - to recall the magic
these hollowed trees - this reverence of sound
so thick with promise - so full of joy
the beating of hearts - the rhythm of drums
I believe are the melodies of life

\#

dreams are not made

they are formed

when there is only dirt

no yellow brick road

when you knew at the start

the wizard was a lie

when you are aware tornados

when applicable to dreams

can be defined as doubt

bundled with fear

and fear

has nothing to do

with rain or storms

and storms are coming

when you order

the number of books

you knew you didn't have

the funds in your account

to remit the amount required

when you run blindly

through the forest

believing the trees

will move

open a path

and guide you

when you leap

as far as possible

from the top

what if there were no titles

of the mountain

knowing the bridge

is invisible

and strong enough

to bare your weight

when you search

the night sky

for shooting stars

not to make a wish

but to pay homage

it stayed

for as long as it could

you are no longer

a dream chaser

or catcher

you build them

from scratch

believing has nothing

to do with

thinking it is so

but has everything

to do with

knowing the manifestation

of necessary will follow you

faith is never blind

it is the

guidance system

of dreamers

who refuse to sleep

\#

some days

the clouds

will rest quietly

undecided if

the tears will matter

won't thunder

or lightning

completely aware

sometimes we are not

good listeners

some days

our attention span

doesn't span at all

love is a puzzle

too often the people

or pieces included

are also puzzle pieces

when our puzzle pieces

are puzzle pieces

we must focus

on the most

important parts

I prefer to start

at your smile

everything else

is secondary

sunshine

can't sun enough

what if there were no titles

to out radiance

how you

make me feel

I can embrace

the sadness

the rains bring

the joy

in the brilliance

of lightning strikes

but nothing

compares

to clouds and you

the best of days

always

has you in them

I am grateful

for the changes

in weather

and thankful

you have the ability

to change my

acceptance

of whatever comes

I prefer

to start my day

at your smile

nothing else

matters

not even clouds

\#

when did it
become acceptable
for mediocrity to be
the replacement
for excellence?
how long has work
been able to withstand
the mirror test
of hard work?
there will come a time
when the things
you produce
outweighs the things
you are thinking
of producing
when will moving
gallantly struggling to force
dreams into form
hold more value
than standing still
by now you know
fairytales always begin
once upon a time
or yesterday
or sometime tomorrow
no one has a way
of measuring your best
or knowing how

what if there were no titles

your best should look

even you

have yet to determine

if you have more more

or a little more best

in you than you

first thought

I pray we will soon stop

speaking in conclusions

painting ceilings

before the walls

and doors are finished

arguments are useless

if there isn't a plan

for both sides

to become better

from the experience

best will never be best

if you have something left

arguments are not over

if you have more to say

or remnants of anger

when you claim

everything is ok

best doesn't argue

or need your voice

as proof

best will always

have a voice of its own

\#

technology can only help
when we have some idea
of where we are going
it is possible to be lost
and not know you are lost
sometimes I find myself Lost
absent from where I thought I was
there are days I discovered
I didn't know where my feet were
I wasn't aware of the direction
my eyes were traveling
you can be lost
and never know you're lost
only to discover your whereabouts
when no one is searching
for parts of you
when the density of silence
grows too thick
when you hear yourself
whimper in the dark
I've been lost before
but not like this
you can't call it found
when your shriek
awakens the neighbors
when after yelling for help
the fire department finally arrived
you can't call it found

what if there were no titles

when you asked them
to come back as though
their laughter was for you
and their smile wasn't still aimed
in the wrong direction
I didn't know I was lost
until you asked me where I had been
asked me where I arrived from
I must've been here waiting
standing so close
to the lost and found
no one knew I didn't belong here
didn't know where I was
or for whom my heart was waiting
I've been lost before but not like this
not like when you found me
limp arms, broken smile, open chest
begging for crumbs of affection
from the one who left me abandoned
accidentally by the lost and found
I've never been found before like this either
never been kissed by a smile so lovely
never heard joy served in a good morning
never knew love without touching
without holding first to see how it fits
I've been lost before but found this time
by hands so gentle I could rest my heart
I could give you me
and not fear ever being lost again

#

what if

I love you

only meant

I believe in you

meant there is

no such thing

as failure

because we agree

to start again

from scratch

if we must

over if need be

change directions

if got to

what if

I love you

meant

I believe in you

even when you don't

mostly when you doubt

always when you fear

what if I love you

meant

I love you

meant

needing you

and wanting you

have become

what if there were no titles

one and the same

meant

all we have

are good mornings

mostly during storms

and around sunset

lunch time

past midnight

what if

I love you

meant

I got your back

when you fall

when standing

seems impossible

when you're tired

of struggling

when the pain

gets unbearable

when you want to cry

when you need to laugh

when you need a chest

to rest your weary

what if I love you

only meant

I love you

and the answer

will always be - E

all of the above

#

I didn't want to write

but I made an agreement with me

I would write every day

even if I feared what I'd say

even if didn't like

where my fingers were going

I didn't want to write a poem today

afraid I would offer too much me

or maybe leave spaces between the thoughts

and you would think I included too much you

thought of writing how I wish too much

how I love too hard or how words

sometimes leap from my chest evading these lips

I wanted to write something that didn't matter

lines of no never mind of pay no attention

wanted to leave me out of this one

poeting isn't easy especially when you learn

your fingers will tell on you

rendering you helpless to stop them

you can find me randomly sprawled about

lying naked between the pages

in the books I've written

thought I hid myself under the covers

didn't think anyone could find me

resting on the table of contents

falling is never fun wish someone

had warned me hearts don't own parachutes

there is no such thing as secrets

what if there were no titles

when you've already walked around
inside of me rearranging my comfortable
swept away my sadness
kicked over the bowl of leftover jealousy
I kept in the back of the freezer
it can't be called a leap of faith
when you've already jumped
when you don't care where you land
hoping a first aid kit is available
when the tumbling stops
when the force of your momentum
comes to an abrupt halt
didn't want to write a poem today
didn't want these words to sound
as though I love you deeply
didn't want me to notice
your absence - can't type missing you
big enough or small enough
to make up for actually missing you
I don't know and didn't ask
where these fingers are taking me
for once I would like to plagiarize
someone who doesn't care
someone who doesn't believe in love
I didn't want to write this poem
didn't want you to discover me
with so much missing you
but at least I kept my word to me
damn this daily write

\#

some days a broken pen

and a bended knee

weighs the same

words when patiently

written down can be

considered prayers on paper

sometimes a shattered heart

a crooked smile, a held back tear

will cherish the same memory

scientist can only tell us

the particles we are built from

not who actually built us

I know the stories of dirt and dust

but there has to be clouds and oceans

mountains and glaciers in here too

I've practiced building thoughts of galaxies

no one has ever told me they saw stars

even the times I've carved pieces

of this heart into a poem

not one of them came

bearing a pulse

it must seem strange

the attachments

our words carry and place

inside of people and things

wanting to show ownership

I've lost enough things in this life

to be sure

what if there were no titles

inanimate objects and people

are only on loan

someone will claim possession

will state time warrants

them custody

I am more writer

of dark clouds than sun

the solemn inference

of knowing pain

of knowing storms

are an intricate part

of our existence

sits silently above us

each cloud filled

with the tales of time

and time will tell us

there is nothing new

just us thinking

we are so much better

than the last group

attempting to master love

and you can be sure

love is its own master

I pray often - sometimes

I think it's only practice

to quit asking for much - to stop wanting

a discerning voice to understand

needs and wants will appear

wearing different emotions

I've never been afraid of love

I know love knows me

and is probably afraid me

I am not aware of my own strength

I think I squeezed the love out of love

a time or two

but that's between me and love

maybe I should sign up for take back classes

I've known those with swift fingers

able to snatch their love back from you

while you watch - you will never know

you won't be aware yours was taken also

I love writing with broken pens

each stroke laced with finality

each word could be a stand alone thought

in a sentence - I pray too often

the longest prayers are those for love

I would prefer to write with bended knees

I must believe the transference of pain

would be of a permanent nature

there would be so much movement

in the making of one word

especially all the curves

and sharp edges it takes to form love

I am either a sitting page

or a walking prayer

even I don't want to know

which category I would find myself in

or maybe I am both

#

dreams are easy to come by
but much harder to keep
friends will want to borrow
yours sometimes... it's ok
even when they steal the parts
they understand that's ok too
your dream will start out a little foggy
it may not be clear for a while
you will know it's yours by the way it attaches
to your palms in a never let go kind of way
doubters will see it too - keep them around
you will require their negatives to test your positives
your positive is where your happy lives
no one can gift you happy you may occasionally
misplace your own every now and again
it is easy to get caught up when things don't go your way
when your present best isn't good enough
when your all doesn't suffice, when you've done all you can
when you have to ask someone else for help
there is a gentlemen inside of you - grow him
into a gentle man - hands are for holding not hitting
helping is easiest when asked - but help those you pass
even if they don't know they need help
even when you're in a hurry to get somewhere
you will grow some better from the process
love is a different matter - I guess because
everyone has a story of it falling apart
of it not working to the plan

truth is... love has no plan and can't fall apart
love is just love we build it good or bad
we all have a tendency of breaking it
of tearing off the rough edges to make it fit
exactly where we thought it should
we think love will work on its own
even when we fail to work it
know this for sure... you can't take it back
once it is given, can't stop loving someone
when they claim to have stopped loving you
no one has the ability to point out your purpose
your purpose has more than likely found you by now
it usually starts out as something you may be slightly good at
better isn't a trivial pursuit - it takes more work than you think
more work than you are willing to put into it at first failure
nothing from this point will be easy
and nothing will be as hard as you were told or think
your best is a mathematical formula you haven't written yet
you will be scientifically adjusting it for the rest of your life
have fun - your fun - don't follow - always lead
or rather find those whose lips and feet fit perfectly
in the sentences formed of the sound they make
I love you more than me - always more than me
I got you whenever you need me to get you
you have everything you need inside of you
have the patience to search yourself first
and second, and third and maybe fourth and fifth
because it may not be visible to your outside eyes
if you don't take your time - take your time

what if there were no titles

nothing is promised not even tomorrows
treat every day with care... this one is new
I've called you sir all of your life
out of respect to practice you respecting yourself
I could always see the king in you
if you respect yourself no one can disrespect you
cursing is ok but practice speaking in sentences
you never know when they will ask you to speak
to presidents, or ceo's or to more students
than the arena occupancy sign allows
I love you more than me - always more than me
you are great already - it is time for you to discover
how much of you you are willing to share
others will see it in you even if you don't
today is the first of many miraculous days - enjoy
remember - you have more work to do
always expect the unexpected but be better on purpose
congratulations, I am proud of you - you honor me
America will treat you as a man now no longer a boy
pay attention to who you allow in your circle
not everyone deserves to be there
don't act as if you're great being great is not an act
follow your dreams - take your time - do your best
are the three rules I offer you to live by
and love - every time give your all
it will not always be appreciated but you can grow a new all
never a second opportunity to give your all a first time
I love you more than me
always more than me

\#

I write for reason

any reason, every reason

to give you reason to be

to speak, to wish, to want

to dream - our bodies are mountains

our voices are the echoes

of what we hear in our heads

of what we feel in the beating

of our chest - words and sound

bear the greatest weight

on our being, in our existence

there is a reason negatives

reverberate more times

throughout our mountain

than positives - they don't fit

can never make our legs dance

they are not a part

of the song we live

are not melodic enough

to be in harmony

anger and smiles

will never be friends

we are heavenly hymns

with background feet

with blinding light for a shadow

we are reason, every reason

any reason, all reasons

let us write for reasons

#

this is not a writing exercise
this is what's done before the stretch
before the exercise begins
imagine you were a pen
or a page or a child
the excitement of the first day of school
how new words carved into a fresh page
at the break of day feels
remember how the second school
you anticipated going to had buses
a new route, a new place
knowing the requirements
of learning would be new
how you paid top dollar
for the new journal
because it looked
as if you could write better thoughts
getting better at anything
takes consistency and repetition
elevating your process
is a practiced method
writing is not a more word thing
it is a better penbrush thing
every blank page is a naked canvas
every pen is a multicolored paintbrush
paint the picture you didn't dream about
you only wish you would had enough channels
to surf through your mind to find

\#

I used to think

a simple

I love you

would suffice

for detailing

my feelings for you

now I know

I live you

will almost explain

how you have

become an intricate

part of my seconds

I don't count

days anymore

I live you

one second

at a time

it took patience

and listening

to every curve

to understand

your beauty

I have learned

and now am skilled

at the process

of tasting

how your cells

are connected

what if there were no titles

\#

do not ask why the storm rages
do not beg the wind to cease
a patient wait for the rainbow
is insignificant - lightning
only arrives in flashes
because it has other things to do
every flood is only trying to find
its way back to whence it came
I have no idea why tornados
dance so magnificently
a hurricane is in a hurry
it doesn't know where it is going
I know these things only because
my pen morphs as the weather
it torments and delights
it is more earthquake than glide
if I fail to hold it tight enough
it could rip my fingers from hands
I don't ask why anymore
I just know these things are true
I am more lightning than hurricane
not rushing any longer
I am completely aware
I have so much more to do
I can write you a rainbow
a storm or write you dreams
while you're awake - that's what writers
are supposed to do - write everything

\#

her words

were enough

I didn't notice

her lips until later

until her silence

stirred the coals

in this heart into a flame

until the heat in my bones

mirrored the sun

until these arms

abandoned my demand

to not reach for her

until her good morning

sounded I love you ish

her words

were enough

made me wish

to be sound

made me want

to be air

when I noticed

she had lips

it was too late

I was too far gone

to close not to ask

for an invite

I invited them

to join mine

what if there were no titles

wanted to hear

their conversations

if they would share

words at all

if they didn't care

about oxygen

if there would be

a secret key to unlock them

wanted to ask if they were magic

had no patience to ask their origin

her lips weren't the kind

I had seen before

I swear she had more than two

I thought they were an army

the way I surrendered

the way my heart

forced its way to her

as if unprotected by chest

ran to her so fast

it must have stolen my legs

when I noticed she had lips

it was far too late

too late to beg for clemency

too late to be pardoned

for the thoughts her lips created

touching them was worth their weight

in elephants, clouds and heavens

all seven of them

eight... if you count her lips

\#

I've met those

with soo much anger

in their throats

every whisper was a scream

every hello sounded

of fist and teeth

you will find no comfort

in discovering smiles

are formed of bones and guts

we would battle for breath

if it wasn't freely offered

some days we fight

just because the sun rose

there must be a place

where peace

doesn't come in pieces

parts of bodies dismantled

where pain isn't love

crushed under hopes ugly feet

I thought love started out whole

not with a hole big enough

to stuff bad memories in

I didn't know our brains

had such giant hands

holding on to things

promised years ago

we would let go of

I didn't know every nerve

what if there were no titles

in our bodies

had an ending

came with limits

anger must be

the monster in the closet

the goblin under the bed

we were always afraid of

I didn't know the dark

wasn't black enough

to see through

wasn't heavy enough to cover

the blemishes life carved

in this skin not blood thick

so emotion thin

love should not be

crime scene beautiful

caution taped for attention

corrections are not sacrificial

shouldn't be given during duress

our tongues aren't perfect

they only move when ordered

words can never fix

the broken ruined by sound

if I sound angry, I'm not

mad means crazy

means I lost minds balance

but this is me finding solace

in solitude - wisdom in a moment

you can lose knowledge

when you're not focused
when love tries to break you
and you have too much love
to be snapped
you've been whole for too long
when you know loves purpose
is to fix the broken
to patch the holes
to heal the sick
I was sick and wasn't aware
love was the doctor
I needed to call - I call love
on a first name basis
I've met those whose intentions
should never be mentioned out loud
who should come wrapped in caution tape
who need to be personally introduced
to love - who should have love on speed dial
I know anger is a real emotion
but can't reside safely in this body
such an unwelcomed visitor
should never be invited for coffee
I am two I love you's from you knowing
I can't be broken - you can't break me
but I can fix you - can repair your broken
I've been broken before
that's the only reason I know
true love
is not breakable

#

I write a poem for me
every earth day
to analyze my truths
not every truth is worth sharing
not every thought is either
but this one is to me from me
reflection has two unique definitions
the mirror test of you
and the memory test of who
you thought you were or used to be
there's a bad guy in here somewhere
don't know why he's not answering
every now and then
I wish he would show up unannounced
he is a boom in a tunnel
a butt naked commando
I will leave it there for now
I know now how to love with all
yet all does not suffice
for the needs of love
I've gotten used to leaving
seeing how fast the backs of those
with forever on their tongues
can disappear - walk away
as though sound was ambient
as if yesterday washed itself with rain
I know what fingers are for
why hands get arthritis

letting go is an art
I am learning to paint it perfect
there are pieces of smiles
no matter how much I shake
they are still in possession
of parts of me
haven't held love or smelled
the after sex aroma
of satisfaction, of laughter
for more than a year
I've never been more happier
with my pen
never been more open
with my truth
never been more sadden
by the things those
I have given my all to
share with
unsuspecting bystanders
in their reflections
of past relationships
in the tales of me
sounding more fictitious
more conjured than truth
I know how hard truth is to swallow
when you are not used to its taste
I am not afraid of dreams or failing
or loving or listening or sharing
I will believe everything you say

what if there were no titles

even when I know it's a lie

hoping this will

be the time

you fool yourself

someone once told me

I need to charge a toll

close the bridge

or damn the lake

passage through this chest

should not this easy

but I have realized

closing your eyes

is not a good thing

when you could

miss a miracle

closing your mouth

at the wrong time

can leave you vanished

closing your heart

could leave room

for lonely to take up

permanent residence

I've learned anger is love

with upside down vision

I've learned pain

is love wearing

too much expectation

I only expect me to be better

for me to lean toward

being the best me

I know how

I have learned how

not to give up

even when forced

to say uncle

made to

white flag surrender

when there is

no more me

left to draw from

I've learned

you don't dream

as much

when you living one

and this dream

is just getting

to the good part

I don't have

closed eye dreams

anymore

because this one

is better than sex

or at least since

it's been a while

it is better than sex to me

happy earth day self

now get back to work

break time is over

\#

I've held silence so tight
it made the earth shake
in a violent quiet rumble
held anger under my tongue
as though it formed a cyanide tablet
my teeth were too afraid to bite into
silence has to be the loudest
of all the emotions we possess
it's impossible to travel
through quiet unnoticed
even humming birds and bees
sound faintly familiar
you will always hear them coming
silence has no warning
no flashing reds or glares
it doesn't sound of arriving or going
it could remind you of left already
I've held silence so tight
it frightened the scream in me
rendered me useless to myself
made me wonder if yelling
would have made a bigger imprint
would have awakened the battle
sometimes wars are fought with tears
every heart beat is a fight for survival
how do you know you're alive
if you don't support the noise of living
if you don't hear yourself scream

even if on the inside

I scream on the inside sometimes

I chant this rally cry for me

evidently life is still bitter

I am still here

still cheering

still dreaming

slapping impossible's

they must be aware

of my plan

to change their name

I carry a mouth full

of imagination

I am still laying

the foundation for

still adding

the finishing touches

to this monuments blueprints

silence will sound of quit

will remind you

of death or darkness

I am built of light

filled with noise

or words it will only matter

to who listens

I had to teach myself

to listen

even when these dreams

grow too big to fit in the ears

what if there were no titles

heaven attached

to this body

my silence

has the volume

of wishes

turned up to max

you will never hear my wishes

only see my dreams

I got extra hands

in this heart

to grip them

when they expand

beyond the realm

of you believing

this dream is mine

I've been silent too long

you will miss my quiet

I always discover

in my every day journey

see it in the complications

of trials

life is angry

with teeth

filled with bitter

that I am holding fast

to dreams

and can't comprehend

why

I am still here

\#

I stopped listening to music

when my dreams quit dancing

when I discovered this heart

needed a jump start

it really gets difficult

when beats disappear

when you require a drum

to start the drumming

when the stethoscope

sounds broken

when nights are silent

when the absence in your chest

means singing solo

means no more harmony or duets

music has been the source

of more than life for me

from Moon River to Blessings

from Bloodstone to Lamar

there were songs intrinsically hidden

in the movement of my day

had to turn the music off

couldn't listen to my own

offbeat rhythms

tears possess a melody of their own

they tap their emotions when falling

and never land where you plan

never sound how you want

I've become more

what if there were no titles

row of empty chairs

for the trumpets and string section

the saxophones and baritones

erased their notes

couldn't play any songs

auto play malfunctioned

auto tunes no longer automatic

had to turn the music off

lost the complete play list

in a fit of desperation

couldn't use these hands

to catch myself

finally found me

sitting in the corner

lonely rock singer

hitting rock bottom

two smashed guitars

every string missing

got too used to big beds

with empty pillows

sheets clean

of memories, of smells

no lingering legs or arms

draped over body parts

I had forgotten

how parts of my body

gravitated to another

how music rested so gently

in the perfection of movement

had to turn the music off

when my dreams quit dancing

when there were no

lip to lip transitions

in the key of love

had to turn the music off

turned the volume to max

there has to be a dance called static

a white noise two step

I'm discovering

undiscovered notes

in my feet

a pattern of hand claps

in these legs

I'm starting to leave the volume on

no longer turning the music off

I'm humming again

maybe off key

reminding me of songs

I once listened to

teaching myself a one man calypso

haven't learned the steps yet

I keep practicing the singing parts

keep losing the melody

my dreams are dancing again

I know I am a symphony

an orchestra of instruments

as soon as I push play

turn the music on... and listen

what if there were no titles

\#

I watched the splash of violence
flick from her tongue and dance in the wind
words cannot create themselves
throats are not equipped with volume control
imagine such destruction exiting the same mouth
once the home of comforting melodies
anger must reside somewhere else in our bodies
if hearts are for loving how than co-exist
I've heard pain was a dance of skulls and bones
it doesn't rest well in our feet
we will break more of our own hearts
than we will ever be able to repair
of those we loan our smiles to
I don't know who said it first
or maybe it was never said at all
we are here for a reason
no one can help you find it
so blaming anyone but you
for losing yours is the tale tell sign
you never had one to begin with
there will be days
we will bless the sun and curse the moon
or curse the moon and curse the sun
and others we would prefer to sleep
praying our closed eye dreams will be a keeper
you must fight for you
if you ever plan to drag the best
from beneath covers

from beneath moments of discontent

you can't call it all

if you have more of you left to give

can't call it gone with your eyes

intently focused on the review mirror

some days left is two steps away

and gone may not need amplification by sound

I remember when we thought

forever was a place we had the address to

when we believed eternity was trapped

between our tightly connected palms

I don't see struggling the same anymore

I don't call my days an act of war

when it's up to me to get the job completed

looking around for help is simply

a luxurious waste of valuable time

sometimes it's the purpose of the ones closest to you

to teach you alone is the yellow brick road

no one else has ever made the journey

to prove to you rocks can be a smooth path

to show rugged is only the way to build a dream

I know it sounds harsh after to death do us part

or the passing of rings

what if we part and still have breath

what if they are just hollowed rounds

what if they are just circles

what if it is up to each individual

to build their own forever one alphabet at a time

what if truth can never be discovered

what if there were no titles

until you take a moment to look it up

there are lessons requiring one for the teaching

asking another to come along may not be a good idea

I wasn't aware of any of this before

it may not ring as truth again tomorrow

now must have some relevance

must be a competent passenger for today

I am learning to no longer place your words

on the scale to see how much they weigh or matter

I would hope we wished the best for each other

regardless how terminally ill relationships become

I have to believe we grow love

as tall and as wide as possible

sometimes it will no longer fit

in the space we placed it to live

love is supposed to continue to grow

whether we water it or not

I need to believe we arrived at this point

for the sake of purpose

some paths are only wide enough

for one traveler - to each his or her own

must be a journey of self

no matter how soft or loud

you tell me to quit running

I am a dream chaser

that's what dream chasers do

we are given determination, will

and energy to run - using everything we have

to chase dreams

#

today is a new day

this one has never

been here before

remove the remnants

of yesterday

from the corners

of your eyes

begin from scratch

building dreams

or anything monumental

starts with planning

construct a sun out of your smile

if you think you need more light

you have everything you need

doubt is never a good companion

when walking clouds

it is a lot heavier than it looks

you got this

we were built for this

do not stress

for instant is usually found

in coffee, rice, bad decisions

and drive through restaurants

neither bids you wellness

even the sun

takes a full cycle

to return to the place

you remember to call day

what if there were no titles

\#

imagine truth

were a bed

of hot coals

and the path

was straight

and narrow

most would rather

take the short cut

through lie

than show proof

of burns

scars are beautiful

especially

when earned

imagine

love was a light

burning at

three times

lightning flash

at least then

you could tell

when there is

no glow

by which

to light

your way

love would be

considered absent

#

broke the shackles

on my purpose

opened my heart

and released my dreams

you have no idea

how it feels to write free

I was taught so many rules

for sentences

they must have treated pages

as prisons

I keep a gang of pens close

ready to attack

every thought attempting to sneak pass

it doesn't matter if eyes

are opened or closed

I have given my mind authorization

to grab hold of anything and everything

we will share

stuff pens full then empty

you have no idea

how it feels to write free

there used to be a cage

I would lock my thoughts in

too afraid of the all

I knew was deep inside

wasn't sure what truth's

would be let out

thought there were

what if there were no titles

secrets worth keeping

I learned subliminally

in every learning institution

naked is for the bedroom

and displayed on statues

I had no idea

how it feels to write free

I was asked what is truth to me?

they asked me to share my truth

I have written more than a thousand pages

of verses and songs truth in everyone

I am more than one poem could bear

more pain and love than any book

could hold or bind together

I must believe truth is the only thing

we were sure would last

would be here after we left

would survive these storms

life tends to be described as storms we survive

not always for the fittest

survival will often be up for debate

you will decide once the rainbow appears

although sometimes I have lost myself

in the glorious shadows of deep brown eyes

in the caverns of heartless beautiful beings

I must believe truth has no eyes

can't see in front of it and has no scale to balance

you asked me to tell my truth

it's impossible to begin at the beginning

I wasn't aware what truth

was in the beginning

I believed what I was told

until it became unbelievable

I must have been around twelve

when someone I trusted

taught me what lies were

they were unforgettably bitter

made me aware

somewhere there must be truth

at eighteen an army recruiter

told the greatest tales

spent the next six years

traveling to find the truth

but I was asked to tell my truth

I always find beauty in a rock

I love too hard - would say fall

too fast or jump too often

I know how empty feels when my all is gone

there is no such place as lost

you've arrived somewhere

you have never been before

hearts can't break but our minds can crack

from the weight of broken promises

every now and then

there are truths I discover daily

and always write them down

I had no idea how it feels to write free

most people are unaware

what if there were no titles

unshackling their purpose

allows it to grow bigger

your purpose can never leave you

dreams will never disappear

you must remember which set of eyes

you last viewed them with

human eyes are faulty

we were never told

our pupils are pupils

we must teach them to see

we mistake blurred sight

for clear vision

forget what you know

search for the unknown

we are filled with marvelous discoveries

we were told we could never find

there is truth in our fingers

we need to share with ourselves

writers block is you

blocking yourself from writing

I was asked to share my truth

my truth is:

I will be here writing

to peel away the covering of safety

others used to shield the truth

life should never come equipped

with safety nets

and I really had no idea

how wonderful it feels to write free

\#

I - born storm

she a hurricane

you will only witness

few hurricanes

without storms attached

we were attached

like category ten's

category tens are destructive

I didn't survive

the coming of shore

we were always

wind and rain

blankets of dark clouds

to remind us

I a mere placer

a rearranger of wind chimes

knew where to place them

to warn of coming storms

together we loved lightning

the sound of heaven - rumbling

mentioning our names

we never noticed

darkness approaching

I - storm - shadow to hurricane

lost myself in the darkness

father to storms

must teach young rains

of hurricanes

what if there were no titles

soon they will be

attached to hurricanes

and may not survive

the coming of shore

I give no warning

just lessons

in the proper placement

of wind chimes

I storm

still in love

with hurricane

can only remember

wind chimes

a language

I never learned to speak

hands fit perfectly

lips touched perfectly

but when receiving

messages

in wind chime

couldn't interpret

perfectly

only knew

it was a sign

of category ten's

some storms

will never survive

the coming

of shore

\#

this morning I tossed
four bushels of thoughts away
before beginning to write
pain is not a great designer of metaphor
anger although nice to meet him
will never be worthy of attaching sound
I watched words I would never use
attempt to crawl into my mouth
lips were as tight as I could keep them
gritted my teeth in hopes
to deter their entrance
my father would tell me
invite them in let them run free
to visit whomever or where ever
they feel they are needed – they only exist
because friends and or family
called them here, needed to witness
a storm, wanting to feel how lightning
can be forced from the lips of a poet
here I sit always choosing
to not give them what they ask
I have been building this better me
for a while now - it is a battle
and centuries of wars to keep him whole
everyone has the intent of dismantling
using their energy to tear him down
I stopped patching the holes years ago
enjoying the rugged look

what if there were no titles

proof in motion life and I
are not always on good terms
but we do dance well together
every time the music starts
I must have thrown away a lot of good ideas
coupled with bundles of blessings
only discovered if I had taken time
to sift through the debris
would've been monumental
could have built a cathedral of dreams
sometimes the smallest snake
has the most harmful venom
I know how my skin responds
when similar sounding syllables
are tossed my direction
I know my ears can't let go of pain
when forced in loudly
I would hate to be the bearer of bad news
often my good news may be bad to you
and sometimes my bad news
is not as bad or impactful as you had planned
I know how divisive love can be
when it breaks
I know how the corners of smiles
will rush downward when you think
forever lost its way - when you believe
someone else captured the heart
you thought you conquered and claimed ownership
I must have tossed some of the best worst

words a mouth can transport to an ear
diffused an earthquake of remorse
buried anger before it was birthed
I am getting better at this new me thing
ego flavored attitudes are a delicacy
it will take years to adapt to their taste
I know what you need me to be
but now I understand what I need me to be
the conflict is not in me - it's in you
I apologize I couldn't sacrifice
the sound you asked for
couldn't negative this positive
I got going on - I am learning
I am not a leader just a follower
of better - a chaser of best
got purpose in these palms
and will not let go
as you fake to shake my hands
you will find out soon enough
as soon as you locate happy in your chest
when you discover good ain't nothing
when side by side with your best
when you truly find out
we are in this life together
even if it appears
apart is the best way to be
there doesn't have to be a we
when life is the same precious
to the both of us

#

some dreams will have enough weight
to wake you - will create such force
will displace years of comfort
you will find moving mandatory
will break out in the fastest sprint
I've dreamed such dreams
felt the uncomfortable misfortune
of actions needing my participation
I've spent years trying to discover
or rather uncover portions of myself
that should be listed as undiscoverable
sometimes explanations are not equipped
with enough sound to make sense
enough meaning to clear internal sinuses
there will always be those too afraid to hear
couldn't fathom if they were paid to
listening is never a given - will not be easy
although ears entrances are clean no debris visible
I have dreamed dreams too large
to fit in the space they originated
couldn't be compartmentalized
in the hall of thought
the arena of confusion was filled with doubt
had to cancel upcoming events
doubt is a lead singer unable to hold a note
hope is not a solo act - it is the conductor
of your orchestra - you are an orchestra
I've always taken for granted

believed the heart is where dreams
are supposed to grow only to learn
you can't grow dreams
your only option
is to build dreams of faith
plastered with perseverance
lathered with enough determination
it can weather whatever storms
come your way - if no one has explained
you have personal storms coming your way
we read of faith having strength
even if the size of a mustard seed
mustard seeds are not for making mustard
they are the biggest example of faith
when placed in the context of mountains
I've dreamed dreams larger than mountains
heavier than the cloudiest of skies
I know how it feels to hold one
and know the pain of watching
a dream break apart at the seams
I know every dream is up to you
so you must be up to conquer every dream
I was told this body was equipped
could withstand the struggles of living
not one person explained
there is a different fight
when it comes to loving
love doesn't always survive - you will
but may not feel you are a survivor

what if there were no titles

\#

what if we

claimed no sect

didn't profess

a connection

to be a follower

of any particular

doctrine

released

ourselves

of titles

we were

no longer hailed

as humans

or men or women

but each morning

we laced tightly

a pair of the same

comfortable shoes

and began sprinting

in every

direction

to catch up

to ourselves

would we not

in essence be

full of life

purpose driven

dream chasers

#

I would conduct
a concerto
in A minor
if I was sure
your smile
would join in
our hearts would be
string section
we would sun gaze
doing the overture
I would love you
to accompany me
in a symphony
of tomorrows
we can
double bass clef
a chorus of wishes
I want to
Rock A Bye Sonata
your sadness
you told me
you tire of songs
no longer wanting
to sing of lonely
tomorrow
will be better
tomorrow
will be brand new

what if there were no titles

\#

this poem will be read in harmony it is written for all of us, me, you, all of us...
for those who have traveled this road before and those hurriedly on their way

there's a bond of silence

sewn underneath the skin I wear

one mention of your name

rip my cells from its intricate lining

releasing the devil in me

and I'm no ordinary sinner

I've played flute and waltzed with Hades

signed redemption a reprieve

gave back my slice of heaven to remain here

hoping you would notice

you reside in places others never knew existed

if I could replace the beating

in my chest with a metronome

you would hear the cadence

of your footsteps in surround sound

for those of you who

have never experienced its taste

jealousy is a mouth filled with black pieces

of a rotten soul apple

and nowhere to spit

its the catalyst

the reason others believe in hate

but hate cannot live here

I now understand the needs of junkies

why elephants travel for days

back to the place

and moment of their loss

I pray to the heavens

for the religious doctrine

to exorcise you from the spirit of me

my only wish - my true hope

is that no one will ever read this

I ordered my disobedient fingers

to stop writing - they refused

I have always been

a man of my word

but you break my tongue

rendering sound

an inadequate gesture

if this life is filled with

twist and turns

why do I picture you

straight and narrow

you are the secret I hide from myself

the blessing and the curse

the tale and the fable

my heart keeps telling

there's a man in here

afraid of his shadow

for even it resembles you

it dances when he walks

it sings in the quiet

imagine this

I'd rather be a slave picking cotton

than in this moment

for you have mastered the best of me

shackled and held captive

the part of me

that has only known freedom

I would call Tubman

if I had the right number

I believe in the space and time continuum

every equation has you as the constant

a priceless variable

an immeasurable azimuth

aiming straight for

the circumference of my soul

I'm just a soul singer

singing country music

a full-house trying to beat four of a kind

the games people play with hearts

have left countries ravaged and war town

I the mere hen trapped in your foxhole of a soul

is wounded beyond repair

there are no questions

just answers looming large

you are the sun cast

on the shadow of my doubt

I've never been afraid of sound

but your ghost screams octaves

shattering the glass shield of my mind

rendering me hopeless and helpless

basking in the thought of you

\#

my mother

would tell me

stories I told her

I remembered

some of them

the others I am sure

my brother or sisters

were the culprit

once

when I was about

five years old

I asked her

for a hug

explained

how great

it had been to spend

this time with her

I can remember

the look

of amazement

she wore

as I began to tell her

I was king of Jupiter

and was only visiting

I loved how

earth children

played and ran about

told her I was sad

what if there were no titles

for my time

was up

she tells

the story

often now

probably

much better

than I did initially

or ever will

my mother

tells everyone

how I would tell

the longest stories

how she had to cook

and clean as though

she was

paying attention

I tell my sons

what my mother says

all of the time now

I bet

I tell her sayings

better than her

better than

I remember

better than

we can

remember

together

\#

there is a space

between dark

and darkness

resting

on the edge

of light

where hoping

with your eyes closed

is the same

as dreaming

while in slumber

purpose requires

movement

failure can only

find you or glance

in your direction

when you

are doing something

when in constant

pursuit of goals

you are

a bigger inspiration

to the ones

you don't know

are watching

than those

you send an invitation

to join in and share

#

there have been nights

it took all my strength

to climb out of

some days I dive

head first into lets me know

I should have worn a parachute

I've been asked to tell my story

how can I? when one sun's passing

may sound of storms for months

comparing days to days is a lesson

I stopped accepting years ago

I got minutes too hard to handle

I learned from every yesterday

as though it was tomorrow

screaming obscenities into my now

just wait until my next gets here

you will see

I can't tell my story

without you believing

I've embellished

made up some impossible's

you couldn't put a match to

if I asked you to help me burn

some of my yesterdays

to the ground

I am just four cold winters

from a potentially great spring

and you're left wondering

why I'm planting

Phalaenopsis Schilleriana

they are just orchids

but why tell you

when you have yet

to believe

anything I've said so far

this fight in me is for me

and days you will never know

almost captured

the whole best of me

I've been told

I was a pacifist

called a man of patience

if you don't know my story

if you've met

at least one of my days

you would call me a dreamer

writer, conjurer of images, poet

I am teaching myself

a masters class

in due diligence

I'm reading volumes

on how to breathe

underwater

I know how drowning

in your problems feel

I know under means

over ain't nowhere

what if there were no titles

to be found

I was asked

to tell my story

wish you had asked

an easier question

ask me where

my positive comes from

while knowing

at least two mountains

will land peak first

somewhere in the

midst of my day

I practice the over under

and through method

because around will

only lead you off path

I know where I'm going

wrote a plan

on when to get there

but most of my friends

helped hell build

this obstacle course

I keep climbing out of

right before first light

I don't own a parachute

trouble is heavy enough

I only have enough go in this back

to carry one rider

I've been dreaming of next

like I know where next lives
like next is just a step away
if I could leap these burdens
If I could drop this trouble
if I could breathe underwater
I could reach next by morning
but this ain't that kind of story
the only good in it
is I am good with it
and that means I am good in it
cause ain't nothing but this bad
to be good in
I still got a couple of yesterdays
screaming obscenities
into my right now
people remain to ask questions
heaven doesn't have answers for
there is one thing I know for sure
I am just four cold winters
from a potentially great spring
and you're left wondering
why I'm planting orchids
it's the hardest flower
to grow
in this
desolate damp
troubled now
and I really
like orchids

what if there were no titles

#

there was a time

we were all open

for those

with good intentions

now we are

closed minded

closed hand

sharp tongue yielders

unwilling to see

the sun at night

if the words

graced you

with enough

luminance

I've petitioned heaven

for more patience

attached to addendum

for more love

I asked

for more everything

I don't know

what you need

to help me

bring back

the good in you

or should it be said

the God in you

I requested

a double blessing

of quiet

so these words

wouldn't hit you

where you hide

your humanity

I am doing

all I can

before I

unpractice

trusting you

you walk

as if you don't

trust yourself

I got you for now

this is no warning

I told heaven

to tell you

to show you

these are

God's words

and God's hands

I had no option

but to share

I would

apologize

but these

aren't

my words

#

my father wasn't a poet
but I leave a pad and pen
beside my bed just in case
he wants to leave a message
or send an angel in his stead
I have come to grips with the fact
these hands, these gifts, these thoughts
these verses of blessings - this voice
have never been mine to keep
I keep mining these talents
keep digging through the depths of me
there has to be more to give
I am here for a reason
my pen keeps telling me
words are my reason
there has to be more of me
I haven't shared enough yet
haven't wrote enough yet
haven't loved enough yet
haven't pained enough yet
there has to more of me to give
I keep giving you the best of me
hoping I can best my best
when tomorrow's better arrive
I stopped writing for play
the day after I stopped playing
I am still here for a reason
for fate's twisted sense of humor

I keep a pocket
filled with laughter
to toss his way
ain't got time to stop
got too much shhh... to do
building dreams
ain't got no easy in it
my father didn't say
it didn't pierce through his smile
being a man and teaching boys to be men
was a battle no one can teach you strategy
time will change your lesson plan
love will make you plan your lessons
in either instance you have to have a plan
and be willing to adjust you not them
time is more intervention than invention
the best you can do is walk as a man should
talk as a man with divine purpose
teach them easy is just an obscure verse
in a hymnal, rap song or words someone
placed nicely in the message of a sermon
I got shhh... to do and they won't understand
until the day arrives and they've got shhh... to do
my father never discouraged my dreams
I am teaching my sons the power of dreaming
dreams are what brought us this far
or rather understanding
you have to build your dreams
in order to make it through

what if there were no titles

one day of trials

I must believe some mornings

the message in my head

came from my father

why pick up a pen

if you don't need to

if he knows I'm listening

willing to listen

I got inspiration on lock down

he never discouraged my dreaming

as a boy I had big dreams

at least I thought

they were big until now

I teach my sons to dream big

clear space if they don't fit

make them bigger than mine

I tell them my father

would want them to dream

to listen to their thoughts

and sometimes

in early mornings

before you realize

where it came from

your grandfather

will pass you a message

will grant you safe passage

to the realm of your choosing

just as long as you believe in you

and keep dreaming

#

I thought time was a doctor
I was told again and again
it is time who heals all wounds
but every time it rains
I feel a saber saw rip open
my chest in the same spot
your fingers, your hand prints
mistook for a festival
you rearranged the contents
removed the glass ceiling
now every time it rains
these eyes betray the liquid in me
I thought my lids were damns
thought lashes were wipers
I remember the last flood
the last glow of moon
that radianced your beauty
how you slowly brushed
gently against my day
if time were a surgeon
these emotions, my memories
would have been
surgically removed
every time it rains
you thunder slap love awake
I hoped it would sleep forever
wished it to slumber
for at least one eternity

what if there were no titles

#

whatever you think you know
may not be what you thought it was
I really couldn't care
would not ask if I did
I just know what I know
there will be days
you have to push aside
burdens dressed as people
or is it people dressed as burdens
know every day there are obstacles
you will not ask to fall at your feet
but will land upright and eyes front
an airport may become your refuge
for more than twenty four hours
it could possibly take longer
your patience will not be ready
for a test it didn't study for
you may be awakened
while resting unpeacefully
on a chair not fit to sit in for more
than ten minutes less known sleep
by a poets opening line... greet him
let him know you appreciated
his psalms, his words in worship
every poem is a prayer
it will not matter who they are praying to
there is honor in the art
you may keep missing your mission

airports are only rest stops

hubs for the wayward traveler

keep moving - today's line for security

will probably be the longest

you have ever seen and thought were possible

be patient - there are more than enough patrons

mouth filled with begging asking the only man

in uniform with no power to advance them

if he could aid them in catching their flight

there is this comradery of verses

poets share in sentences out loud

so hearing AJ you are supposed to be in this line

wasn't shocking - just know you are

where you are supposed to be

there are lessons you will need

to place in the same pocket you keep your pens

to write when the time comes

you will not be aware the time is coming

standby is what it is when flying

you won't know until lift off

if you are the one left standing by

I wish I had made this up

conjured this story out of imagination

but the next flight was the same

I happened to be the last to board

landing more than 50 miles from home

is only comforted by the word home

understanding time has the ability

to be on your side can only be understood

what if there were no titles

when discovering time has no sides

next there was a bus, a train, a train

another bus and a bus that seemed

to wait on my arrival at each station

followed by walking about 3 miles

there will be days you are aware

your journeyman needs to be awakened

enjoy the excursion 107 degrees may greet you

welcome you home - acknowledge it

keep moving - life wouldn't be life

if there were no lessons in your days

requiring your pen to make note of

how can you write joy

and not sweat through the pain

I don't know what you think

I really couldn't care

I just know what I know

and write what my mind tells me

this journey of discovery

doesn't involve me knowing

I am the scribe of lessons

a closed book open to learning

every day is new - the glare of the sun

greet it - if the moon shows up

bask in its glow awaken your journeyman

live as though it matters write as though

you know time is on your side

understanding all the while

time doesn't take sides

\#

every day

is a fight for survival

sometimes I have to wait

until tomorrow gets here

to determine

if I am still breathing

if I survived or won

ain't no way to tell

there are no winners here

it's just winters here

people can be so cold

like ice or frostbite

you'll never know

until your toes fall off

or can't find your coat

to cover a heart

surrendered for the taking

a heart attack doesn't mean

the beating stopped

it signals your heart

is under attack

there are those

who will ask you for all

not aware

how heavy it can be

love ain't free

and can't be weighed

or held comfortably

what if there were no titles

while walking or running away

most will run away

when love beats

the rising of a new sun

when it stays past darkness

you will not know if you survived

until tomorrow comes

until you check life's gage

to see how much you

remains intact

I've been surviving

on prayers and hope

ain't no nourishment

in prayers or hope

faith and doubt are tasteless

no matter how big

the bite you've taken

which direction it pulls

or tugs violently on your days

some days it will be

about surviving, staying focused

on the promises you've made

you will have to promise yourself things

you don't know if you can keep

you will not own hands enough

to hold on to

and no safe space for keeping

there is power in the word

we survive on the sounds we make

the voice will not be yours

what we receive are echoes

bouncing off closed minds or mouths

we seldom listen to the things

spewing from our cavernous throats

navigating out of our own way

is the hardest part

you can't know

the obstacles were built by you

from uncertainty

from practicing

blocking blessings

you were told

were trails or lessons or karma

blessings are never gift wrapped

most of them have pain for a shell

looked tossed away

unwanted and ugly

no one wants to be

tossed aside or unwanted

you will have to promise yourself things

you don't know if you can keep

surviving is your only job

what if tomorrow

doesn't arrive in time

what if your yesterday

is still breathing

imagine you have a belly filled

with desires un manifested

what if there were no titles

hoping can lull you to sleep

make you think

there is power in dreaming

not it the building of dreams

a fist full of want will eventually

turn into need if you hold it

tight enough, long enough

some wishes will snap quicker

than the bones

broken to make them

you can't survive on wishing

hoping and praying

doesn't require work

you have to work to survive

breathing is a battle

you didn't know

you were fighting

I have these things

called fingers

griping pens as weapons

it is how I learned to survive

I can write anything

the sun

a coat for warmth

but can't write winning

because ain't no winners here

it's just winters here

and people even those

closest to you can be so cold

#

just because
you haven't scuffed
the heels of his or her shoes
still doesn't mean you're not
following too close
we haven't read enough history
haven't studied enough of the past
to see where the road leads
we've chosen to travel
there are words given new meaning
when we were not paying attention
and failed to ask when and why
such changes were needed
we say my click as if the connection
is permanent forgetting seatbelts
unfasten just as quickly
making the same sound
therefore clicking in any form
or definition is temporary
lasting only as long as it takes to arrive
it may sound great to label
men and women after our favorite pets
back in the day calling musicians cats
was a way of pointing out
he or she had their own style
added a bit of specificity to the art
it wasn't necessary to follow or lead
all you had to do was blend

what if there were no titles

and be sure to stay in your lane
the term my dog leaves room
for discernment, requires a further explanation
for dogs don't always finish
in context of being man's best friend
they are not as loyal as you read
in books printed by the SPCA
some will runaway the first chance they get
others will not come to you
when you call them
using whatever name
you believed would befit it
some dogs have a history
of biting their owners
when they least expect it
we have become skilled
at embellishing any story
I know you've noticed it too
on all of the latest movie trailers
a small caption appears
"based on a true story"
so getting your new friends
to not like your old friends
is relatively easy, do not add your part
in the why's, don't mess up your image
splitting hairs on the insignificant details
give only your version of their side of the story
that part of history we have learned all too well
remember Iran and the search

for weapons of mass destruction
we found out early
they were none existent
it would've saved so many lives
if the war ceased at this great discovery
or rather non discovery
but it wouldn't save face
and saving face is why we are here
why we lie in the first place
why truth never rings or sings
as good as the lies we make up
making ourselves look better
in the worst of light and bad angles
we've become masters of upholding our image
even when we are left
with no image at all to hold up
what if we stopped doing it America's way
if we are in need of a new word
we create it ourselves
no more flag placing, confiscating words
unable to defend themselves
leave them be - they are still in survival mode
from the first time they were stolen
maybe if we learned to stand
in someone else's feet
it would make clear the position
we've placed them in
and we are very skilled
of placing ourselves in the best of position

what if there were no titles

\#

ashes to ashes

dust to us

we are of dirt

and earth

no one need know

the legend of our roots

I remember saplings

watching you grow

wishing you and I

were planted together

you are blossom to me

here in this place

where Autumn is a war

we lose every season

you are season to me

every season

I will hold you close

we can reach

for sun together

I stopped wishing

when we met

stopped wanting

when you arrived

stopped needing

when you held me

you hold me

as close as bark

I will sacrifice soil

if you require

more earth

to grow

our union

created

more saplings

our roots

run deep

together we are

crown high

no one need know

the legend

of our roots

you are the root

of my beginning

my branches

will never let go

you are season

to me

every season

to me

we will teach

our saplings

of love

of beginnings

of seasons

every season

they will also sing

our earth song

what if there were no titles

\#

early in the morning
may not be the best time
to ask if you still feel
the way you felt
before this one arrived
I had hoped my voice
has an echo, a twin
would repeat itself
automatically when doubt
makes you question
makes you wonder
if those questions need answers
if you need to re know something
I have said enough times
to not let you forget
I know how change preys
on unsuspecting hearts
how beats drown our memories
how we lose ourselves in ourselves
when pain shows up unannounced
I am a walking tourniquet
a barrel of life sized band aids
I will give you all of me
to catch the parts of you
life will break off
will leave dangling in the wind
I am willing to tie myself around you
if you need me to - if you ever forget

I will bend time

so you will remember

I've watched thoughts leak

from those before who knew

I offered myself to them

as in ancient times

a sacrificial lamb

to bear their burdens

we forget how to share

so used to being alone

we find comfort in the quiet

I know in the early morning

is the best time to ask

before we become aware

this one may be dark

could bring old storms to a new day

could anvil our bodies in sadness

we were not prepared to carry

this much weight

there will be days we wait to see

if a smile we greet us

before we smile at ourselves

we lay every emotion on the table

ready to pick the one we need

to mask ourselves with

if you ever forget how much lots is

how big my all fits you perfectly

if you happen to not remember

the thousand I love you's

what if there were no titles

I tore from my chest

and grew for you just yesterday

if you ever forget

some nights are stallions why ride a mare

when it could never get you to now

love told me to stop here until you arrived

you appeared as it said you would

I wouldn't be looking

but would know it was you

by the way your words were magnets

to these knees with no metal

how they bend thanking heaven

God must have made this plan we

to alleviate any options of a plan b

I find myself missing you

but quick to remember

you reside inside of me

so how I can miss myself

if you ever forget how love feels

just touch me and you will know

how much lots is - how my all

my everything fits you perfectly

even if I tried to forget

or not remember

love told me to wait right here

you arrived just as it said you would

I would know it was you

by the empty I felt

when you became my all

#

I don't know
what you think you know
or what you thought you heard
haven't a clue what you were told
to get you here
poetry for some is their life force
it is the reason some of us live
it can literally save lives
there are times it can boost your ego
to sizes too large
for the human body to carry
we build words as houses
wondering why we can't live there
I know poetry can soothe
the savage beast and create a beast
out mild mannered civilians
we cannot believe we will outlive
our words or our words will live
longer than the motion or sound
used to give them form
it is impossible to write and not get bitten
by your pen every now and then
you will cut yourself to supply more ink
you will think your best work is a foot
only to discover tomorrow is not here yet
you will sometimes find a rainbow
discarded in a dumpster
an abandoned halo on skid row

what if there were no titles

nothing is impossible

when you are aware

of the possibility

you can write everything

or nothing finding everything in it

you can create truth out of a lie

or write a lie into truth

it will not balance the equation

I know how hard it is sometimes

to make an angry pen

carve glad tidings into a page

or how to form smiles

out of a flood of tears

I've been there and will

probably revisit soon

I know how words

can manifest themselves

out of clouds or wind

how rain sounds when it speaks

how silence can be sentence worthy

I don't know what I think I know

or what you were told

to get you here

I just know

we are both supposed

to be here writing

trying to build a mansion

we will never

be able to live in

#

there are no lessons in keeping

we practiced as babes

the pulling up

the heavy handed touching

most of us mastered

the holding on

it started with things

we were given

we didn't want to give back

afraid the giver

would change their mind

always sticky fingers and dirty hands

we weren't aware our hands were dirty

we didn't care - if keeping was the end result

I often wish love was tangible

wish it had body or volume

wish it were a candy cane or jolly rancher

wish I could place my fingers around it

I learned years ago holding on

but not to love – love wasn't something

you thought had the potential

of anyone taking it back

someone loving you is no longer for keeps

I don't know how to make it stay

begging will leave you needing more

hoping will damage your faith

if it fails to work

wishing is a broken bone or fairytale

what if there were no titles

we stopped reading during adolescence

I used to believe in love

knew loving is why we are here

understood giving all

would make you better

I don't believe anything in this world

is for keeps anymore

especially love

I've watch it vanish

dissipate into thin air

right in front of me

watched it curl up into a ball

and bounce away

there are more lessons

in running away

than there are in keeping

I've tried keeping

while watching love leave

practiced staying long after

love had gone

there are no more forever's

no more eternity

no lessons for keeping

just lessons in listening

hoping not being able to hold

not being able to keep

doesn't catch you off guard

sometimes left has no sound

all that remains is quiet and gone

\#

I asked God for you

not someone like you

or someone who looks like you

I literally asked God for you

I've spent a lifetime studying

how God answers prayers

this time I heard heaven

say your name

it always comes in threes

I heard heaven say your name

three times, then there was thunder

after God speaks He always

ends the message with thunder

I believe that's just a heaven thing

you don't know how long I prayed for you

how every night I grew a better description

after years of no answer I decided to draw

knew I needed to paint a perfect picture

since the others were great imitations

didn't know in the beginning

no one knows in the beginning

it always starts with a feeling of real

I didn't want to dive in the ocean

while waiting on the cliff

He told me to told to stand

the diving part was His idea

it always seems love and falling

goes hand in hand or heart in heart

what if there were no titles

either way I knew there was jumping

knew the leap had to be voluntary

when I first refined my prayers

I knew designing your hair

would take at least three nights

a pen, pad and dictionary

can't explain why everything

when dealing directly with heaven

will always have three parts

three days, three ways of saying

to alleviate the possibility

of having three different meanings

I defined the intricate details of your hair

in ways only heaven can understand

I told Him to give it the glory

the same glow of the burning bush

how Moses was too afraid to approach

it had to be breathtaking and beautiful

make it curly as though it could lock

if it wanted to lock, give it the texture of stars

in dreams I touched one so I would know

how it felt when you got here

I didn't describe your body

for heaven has always mastered

the building of elegant structures

but hearts require so many details

at least three months or three years

of directions, of remembering the best

of recalling the most needed qualities

love or is it hearts

are a balancing act

a perfect concoction

of want, will and need

I've watched hearts crash

and burn too many times

I think some of the ones

I placed my love in before

the backdoors were removable

latches were too loose

I don't know how or where

love leaked out - but it did

I asked heaven to make

this heart of faith

tested in the depths

of the wettest pain

the kind waves can't shake

and storms cannot climate

I don't know how faith feels

but it has the strength of legend

of everything we believe could last

give it the power of conviction

the assurance of a couple of eternities

connect it to a smile

just as Jacob wore

when wrestling angels

this smile has to be the same

as Noah held on to when dark clouds

began running across the clear midday sky

what if there were no titles

let this smile bear the blessings
as the rock in the dessert
giving life whenever
dehydration is inevitable
I prayed our feet, knees and back
be reinforced while dragging
this complete set of luggage
filled with lessons and trials
we are not sure we made it through
I repeated twice more
the blueprints for your smile
its complicated explaining
why everything when dealing
directly with heaven
will always have three parts
I asked God to send me you
you are the three parts of me
I've been missing
even I wasn't aware
three parts were missing
heaven knew
you would complete me
I am not for sure
how heaven knows
I just know heaven knows
then comes the clear sky
and loud burst of thunder
after God speaks - He always
ends the message with thunder

\#

there will always be

a morning sun

sometimes clouds

will try and fool you

there will be a moon

for our nights

even when not in view

you will never know

how many stars

shine long after

their fire has dissipated

it is easy to find anger

when going through the war of days

lessons are tools for teaching

believe me life is a better teacher

than we can ever be students

I am learning much of me

needs much of you to exist

we are in this together

when apart appears to be

the best way to us

all I know is every day

this all in me must be expended

to expect a bigger all tomorrow

and tomorrow, yea tomorrow

I will be better at this all thing

I have to

yeah, I really have to

what if there were no titles

\#

I didn't fall in love with words

in the beginning

I think it was alphabets

simple strokes requiring muscle memory

and the smooth curve of numbers

along with a thick round pencil

seemed to so fit well in young hands

big chief tablets became my best friend

maybe I failed to use the whole page

who does when there are so many pages

requiring attention - I discovered elegance

in the movement of fingers

my mother never asked... but I knew

she didn't understand

why I carried the two of them everywhere

big chief and thick red pencil

my family were singers - mother a pianist

music in my life began early

the melody of a dull knife and pencil

lead was never happy - never stayed sharp

I wrote for the sake of writing

had too many arguments with borders

to stay inside of them

it was a small hands big idea thing

should have thrown a celebration

the day I learned vowels and sound

felt of kisses - felt magical escaping my lips

I knew then we would be inseparable

the day I discovered pens I had no idea

pencils could be so jealous

I would see them lying about

everywhere I looked - they must've tried

in every way possible to regain our friendship

I decided to keep one with me for memories sake

pens possessed an endless flow

I could write for days and never need a knife

I wasn't aware at the time but Dr. Seuss

taught me poetry - showed how words

had the potential of dancing on their own

how alliteration was musical

can't remember exactly when

I fell in love with pain

or rather love - now days

you will seldom see one

without the other close by

my mother sung

'Somewhere Over the Rainbow'

and 'Moon River'

I wrote of rivers and rainbows

couldn't tell the difference

I think I fell in love with words

the day I found words mattered

I wrote and they spoke back

hummed and the words became songs

they meant more later

than the moment they were given life

I can only remember when pencils

were my favorite - when big chiefs

held the best of my emotions

the melody of dull knife and lead

when we were inseparable

big chief, pencil and I

no matter how crooked the letters

or how misspelled the words

pencils were my first love

you never forget your first love

I didn't fall in love with words

in the beginning

it must've been alphabets

it still feels the same

words and I - pens and I

with whatever paper I can find

no longer depending on muscles

to remember or recall

even now I have this great affinity

for sound - words resting

snuggled affectionately on my tongue

feels magical, feels of kisses against air

more love now than in the beginning

I will tell my seeds the story of pencils

how pens are not better - how words are music

how loving anything you must give

your true focus and constant attention

I had no idea pencils could be so jealous

they are still my first love

and you will never forget your first love

#

in order to write your truth

you must prepare yourself

the weight will be unexpected

it will always be accompanied by doubt

doubt is much heavier

than any truth you will discern

sometimes you find

or may not find what you've lost

or looking for or told was there

sometimes the discovery

may be too early

or a couple of years too late

it could be right on time

but your watch is absentminded

time is a winged creature

we can never catch

or hold in place for too long

is as elusive as a breeze in a raging storm

I still have every piece and remnant

of every dream from the beginning

from the day I was made aware

of the possibility

you can make them come true

we never start out knowing

could be no one knows or knew

how to care for or hold one properly

you can't grab a dream tightly

as if it belongs to only you in the beginning

what if there were no titles

we thought we could use hands

for everything

even the delicate form

dreams take at creation

are too fragile for fingers

too invisible to share with those

not conscious enough

of how dreams are supposed to look

the fact is… you can't embrace a dream

until you are able to seize your whole truth

neither will be familiar

more than likely

you won't have cents to pay attention

or sense to pay attention

there is only a short bridge

between our conscious

and subconscious mind

we seldom pay the toll to cross

I was asked if I could recall

my closed eye excursions into darkness

if sleep was where I found my purpose

if I found my dreams in dreams

some questions didn't arrive

to find truth as an attachment

there is an apology in here somewhere

I keep erasing - and remembering

to delete, to remove - to hide

some pain may not be removable

it won't be pain anymore

when it finds residence

in your bones

I keep trying to write truth

in a country flooded with lies

some questions will never be asked

to find truth as an attachment

there is this dream I keep finding

locked in the neck of an empty bottle

saved from my father's drinking days

or discovered on a page or folded corner

in the back of my mother's bible

these may be considered scriptures

when you read them to yourself

when no one is listening

to yours eyes

I keep trying to write truth

it doesn't fit well in the opening

where sound escapes

can't sit still while this tongue

moves at a velocity faster than light

I got days I've been holding for weeks

and years stashed in memories

I am afraid to open around friends

I got truths you can have

first you must prepare yourself

the weight and volume of words

will be completely unexpected

there won't be any doubt

I don't do doubt

what if there were no titles

\#

we are all accidents

waiting to happen

skin covered boxes

trial and error included

struggling to get this purpose

this goal, this dream thing right

waiting for a miracle or a blessing

whichever comes first

none of these days are our to keep

although we believe the sun

rose over the planet just for us

we are either geniuses

suffering from Alzheimer's

or fools allergic to logic

speaking more than we need to

knowing less than we were taught

walking when life demands we run

every morning is a dance

we forget to bring the music

there are train tracks

beside my grandmother's house

every day she told their story

every day was different

she taught me every day

should be different

the sky holds firmly billions of stars

that learned to glow long after their flame

has ceased to burned

tell me it's an accident

tell me it's on purpose

it doesn't matter it happens

there is a life line in my palms

only God can locate its end

I try explaining to my sons

I've learned everything by accident

and it is up to each of them to understand

nothing happens by accident

the problem is this language was stolen

part borrowed maybe bartered

I can never get it right

they didn't get it right

my grandmother said

there is blood on those tracks

we can no longer see

of men who worked there

from sun up to dusk

died there attempting to make a living

needing to feed their families

doing the work men are supposed to do

she told me this is what purpose

sounds like - she asked me

to try and imagine the struggle

the fight for survival

none of it is an accident

we live on purpose

we love on purpose

we are geniuses by accident

\#

imagine

our bodies

were a continent

our hearts

were an ocean

one kiss

can create a ripple

affecting our days

as the waves

of change bounce

from the shore

of our thoughts

once I tried

to love as the sky

wish I could

invite you in my

chest to rest

storms will come

every drop of rain

has a purpose

I must believe my purpose

is to comfort you through

the ripples of life

I will always be shore to your ocean

no matter how tumultuous the wind

I can kiss you a rainbow

in the middle of a storm

or on the eve of every cloudy day

\#

I don't count days
I go by the number of
crescent moons
nights without much light
I'm creating a theory of missing you
you're the sun in days of storms
the glow in my twilights
the curve in my smile
you probably weren't aware
of all the things tumbling
around inside of me
at the very thought of you
even your name resonates
my heart to decibels of happy
I am creating a theory of missing you
but I need you with me
to compile all the necessary scientific data
no theory is complete
will ever be complete without the application
to real days in real time
you've become my reason
for doing - for being
for laughing - for searching
for solutions to the dilemma
of suffering through minutes
without your presence
missing you is real and not
a proposed theory for scientific discovery

what if there were no titles

\#

over time I have learned there is nothing God created stronger
than the bloodline, more powerful than the flow of life
through our veins - this is the ultimate source of glory
of blessings, why God made love, emotions we spend our lives
attempting to discover, the same powerful love transferred
from our ancestors to our grandfathers and grandmothers
to my mother and father, from my soul to my seeds
the same love we share as family
through thick thin - through bends and breaks
through love and hurts - through our mistakes
through smiles and cheers - through love and tears
from sea to shore - through all these years
we've watched how time can take its toll, the loss of love ones
as time unfolds, we gather together the young and old, to share our love,
to give our souls, If you ask me why I am still here
it's in the love we share year after year
we will teach our seeds - what family needs
show the legacy of our family tree
over time I have learned there is nothing God created
stronger than the bloodline, more powerful than the flow
of life through our veins - this is the ultimate source
of glory, of blessings - why God made love - this emotion
we spend our lives attempting to discover, the same powerful love
transferred from our ancestors to our grandfathers
and grandmothers to my mother and father from my soul to my seeds
we are love - we are life, we have pains - we work through strife
through all of these through all our seeds
we find everything we need in FAMILY

#

if I could peel away

layers of skin

for every forever

ending in a yesterday

if I could measure

the volumes of tears

shed for all the eternities lost

if I could take back the audio

erase the lies fed by

the prettiest lips

the tearing away

of memories

would be endless

I've witnessed happy

having a timeline

while watching faith

reach its limits

you don't know how words

mean more to me than people

and how people use the words

that means so much to me

as though they dissipate

into nothing

after being released

I can still hear the forever's

that didn't last past yesterday

and won't be here tomorrow

I know how thin this skin is

what if there were no titles

it doesn't protect

from the elements

it barely covers these bones

I can't remember if I ever

believed in forever's

they sounded

so easy to follow

fit perfectly in the place

I used to hide my happy

until it burst

out unexpectedly

now it won't leave

it cries too much

my happy knows

trials can't effect it

I have discovered

if it doesn't hurt my frame

it can't destroy my happy

today

I started writing

a personal blueprint for forever

it will begin with good morning

no matter what time of day

maybe some eggs

a cup of coffee

maybe not

could be just coffee

there is magic

in a good morning

followed by a cup of coffee

or the smile before the first sip

no one knows how long forever is

I will good morning you

until it gets here

I will cup of coffee you

until you smile at empty cups

until you know

I keep coffee stored

in the lining of these lips

I see forever in your eyes

no one knows

how long forever is

but I will gaze into yours

until forever

notifies us it is here

I am now satisfied with this skin

how a band aid can stop the leaking

how tightly it covers these bones

how our bodies kiss

all over at once

I don't know how long forever is

or how heavy the words rest

when spoken into existence

I just know I am willing

to good morning you

to cup of coffee you

until forever acknowledges

we have arrived… good morning

\#

when you finally write the poem
you've been scratching
through your skin to find
biting your lips to swell
praying your mouth
too injured to open
you have ripped at these thoughts
every since you learned
pens are the best friends
with whom to yell your secrets
when you search for a covering
to hide the holes in your soul
you dug and clawed the words from
its ok to tell anyone who sees
these are battle scars
you don't know my war
when you share sentences
or read aloud the verses
you've been too afraid to release
you will not hear applause
there won't be smiles from listeners
their eyes will refuse to look into yours
do not worry this battle is also for them
most are weary of pain
won't even pinch themselves
cannot fathom where this comes from
will believe you haunted their sleep
will consider you a thief

a junkie of woe - its ok

there is a place we meet

between heaven and hell

while we are told we slumber

forty winks can be a prison sentence

if you fail to pay attention

if you don't know why you rest

there is no rem or remembrance

no one will know they were included

accept the blame or burden

whichever you choose

no time for explanations

this will not be the last

it's just the first time it happened

the next will be more painful

you may require a shovel or back loader

beg for a release valve

you will need a new pen

most weren't built to hold

this many secrets

you will have to find good

in your worst days

discover better in your best

you will not be aware there is a difference

until you learn the power of writing

truth is a sledge hammer

sometimes too heavy to lift

some days you will drop it on your own foot

truth hurts - you can strain your back

what if there were no titles

trying to move truth

with no one noticing

I have a body filled with gashes

unpatchable craters

thoughts fall out of

these verses constantly

force my soul to discharge

freedom is the ability

to not choose who listens

to not pick the ears

to let everything land where it may

I keep scratching at scabs

I know more should arrive soon

always finding good in my worst days

most of these are pretty bad

if not for all the pens

I share my secrets with

and packed pages growing weary

from bearing the weight of life's lessons

I would have perished long ago

got to keep moving - keep screaming

ain't no peace here it's just pieces here

I will spit until my mouth heals

until the swelling in my lips cease

until I find the right covering

there is a battle in verses

most are tired of seeing

and listening to the sound

of open wounds

\#

I've been writing eclipses

carved deeply in black on black

pages of chance

a winter solstice on leave of absence

a crying sun dripping lava for tears

hell on earth no longer metaphorical

scars refuse to heal when it's the home of hearts

you have no idea how hard it is

to find your fingers

when your hands are missing

when two arms are not enough

to lift the crown of clouds

I'm wearing half of a shadow

standing under a darkened moon

a broken chalice of hope

is impossible to sip from

don't ask me how I got here

when I am leaving or when I arrived

I woke up like this

or dreaming this dream of being here

either way I'm writing poems in morse code

praying to discover the perfect smile

at the end of the beeps

left a trail of breadcrumbs as a map

fairytales are not a good place to start

end or visit

can't let anyone know I'm lost

or found or bewildered

what if there were no titles

I have a head cold

in my pen or a pen cold

in my head, healing requires

the movement of thoughts

the persistent motion of pens

writing in sniffles and sneezes

a process I've grown accustomed to

poetry is not only what I do

being an artist of words

is who I am

I wish I could print

me out in word

photoshop my life

in pdf format

I write in pictures

that should be paintings

or paintings

that should be pictures

or people or both

can't explain how complicated it is

finding your fingers

when your hands are missing

trying to dance with no legs

when arms don't own strength enough

to drag your body from the abyss

from the residue of despair

poems can't quite speak

for themselves

sometimes sound

will be void

of the texture

voices attempt

to maintain

I am simply

a lily pad

who misplaced it's pond

a frog kissing princesses

just because

he loves kissing

you don't know hurt

if you've never lived

through pain

I haven't a clue

how to place

scars properly

into verses

so I'll keep

carving deeply

into black on black

pages of chance

one day soon

you will discover

these etchings

my prayer

is for faith

to awaken hope

and send it

scurrying my way

#

it won't be easy
but to live your dreams
a bit of self-surgery will be required
cutting your legs off
while maintaining a clear mind
to attach them to your dreams
enabling them to run
is much harder than you think
disbelief, anger and doubt
are not sutures
able to hold anything together
for any length of time
use your bones for thread
how you place them
through the eye of the needle
is up to you
I hate tell you
but pain is a part of the process
you will lose friends
associates, family, yourself
or at least parts of you
no one will understand
not even you
your follow through
has to be formidable
even your shadow
will be cautious
of tagging along

#

last night

I wrote this in the dark

wanting to capture how it feels

at the peak of day when you're not here

how it feels missing you

the extra weight of silence

the pain of wanting you near me

my midnight needs your company

I don't recall ever needing

not this way, not like this

thoughts become much heavier

can't explain how your smile

rushes in, how your voice comforts

the boy in me he's been asleep

for as long as I can remember

I can feel him

running through my body

to greet the sound of you

since you've entered my heart

wishing has become nonexistent

I only use hope, you and forever

in the same sentence

I dream of you

every prayer begins with you

I am not sure of much

but you are the blessing

I've waited all my life to receive

I only say I love you

what if there were no titles

because there are

no other words

if I could I would

give you me as sacrifice

I love you like old testament

like angels marched

around my heart

for three days playing trumpets

until all my defenses collapsed

until I surrendered my all to you

I didn't know it were possible

to love this much

to lose myself in your gaze

every day I wait to see your face

pinch myself as proof you are real

I find myself begging God

to insure you love me as you say

I thank heaven for sending me you

I pledge allegiance to you

Dear Faye Marie Hanshaw

I love you with all of me

you are the poem

I try with all my might

every day to write

and discover happiness

because I know it's impossible

so I will love you every day

for you are my living breathing

poem - you are my poetry

#

when you get used to pain

it will become rather comfortable

hiding in the marrow of your bones

you won't know it doesn't belong to you

scars are reminders of battles

it will not be of consequence

to note winners or losers

we have carried the same scars

reopening them after first impact

familiarity with pain

doesn't make us family

we will grow old

trying to rid ourselves of lessons

pain and trials often reflect

the same image in the mirror

there are mirrors in our days

we won't be prepared to face

some days we will not agree

with the selfie starring back at us

we were not meant to take selfies

wearing pride as outside attire

does not beauty make

although we are all beautiful inside

building a nation requires more hands

than attached to the arms our bodies own

we act as if we are individual countries

or each person is a nation

flaglessly pouting independence

what if there were no titles

being privileged is having something

you didn't earn not caring of its origin

or which member in your linage

took time to remove the bloodstains

I remember the first time I met pain

it traveled closely behind a lie

could it be pain and lies are the best of friends

we all know love and hurt skips together

holding hands while marching through relationships

I can recall the first time I met hurt

she was about five feet three inches tall

heart made of sledgehammers

would drop it every so often on my smile

could be the marrow in my bones

would miss pain if it were ever to leave

the best lessons are those containing

the strongest blow to our egos

the reason pain was created

is to wake us from sleeping

to force our conscious minds to pay attention

how else would we know we are alive

for years we have practiced mastering mask

while suffering from blanket syndrome

using laughter as the shield and the biggest smiles

to barricade our disappointment

there are few remedies for pain

some days you won't notice it is there

and others it will be the only thing

you think about

\#

which weighs more?
the problem someone
brings you or the struggle
you've been carrying
most bodies only have two arms
two hands and one mouth for a reason
you can only speak of one problem at a time
hands are not able to hold much weight
some burdens are birthed with no handles
it took more than a year for your legs
to get used to bearing one frame
you would think by now it is easy
walking in someone else's feet
wearing another's throat
mimicking their sound
using your lips to echo
things you have no knowledge of
each new day arrives
with its very own adjustments
the earth could be rotating faster
or a tad bit slower
time may be unwilling to pause
giving you the opportunity to catch up
your shadow may not feel
the walk in necessary
you could be alone in this
some familiarity with numbers
will be required to count

what if there were no titles

the external body parts you have

you are never alone in this

you may have discovered

somewhere in your past

you couldn't depend on you

this is a new day

tell yourself your problems

take notice did you turn away

or try and leave

we seldom depend on us

to get us through

always asking someone else

whose battles you haven't a clue

if they are winning or losing

if life is not a game

why do we label it

winning and losing

it should be about surviving

about making a better

impression on yourself

imagine you were proud of you

not to the point

you didn't need or crave

the fellowship

companionship of others

you now have faith in your ability

you believe you can handle

the obstacles you are confronted with

your throat is yours

you have your own voice
you stopped trying
on someone else's feet
even your shadow
walks with you in the dark
I know how hard it can be
when everyone you helped
was there only because
they needed your help
not your friendship
if you do for others
expecting a return
on invested time
or efforts
you are doing
for the wrong reason
if you can help others help
if you can't help them
help them find help
some people
are put on this earth
as a directional arrow
to aid others in finding their way
you will never be alone in this
most bodies have two arms
two hands, two legs, two feet
two ears and one mouth
for that specific reason
you will never be alone in this

what if there were no titles

#

she

asked

what I

thought

so I

told her

the truth

I remember

the first time

I was told

it were

possible

to place

your most

sincere wishes

on shooting stars

when asked

to make a wish

I wished for you

when my cousin

explained in detail

if two people

held each side

of the breast bone

of a chicken

pulled until

it was forced

to break

the person
holding
the longest
piece
wishes
would
come true
each and
every time
I held
the longest
piece
I used
all my wishes
and wished
for you
I asked her
would she
allow me
the pleasure
of loving her
forever
her reply
how long
is forever
my response
from
right now
until then

what if there were no titles

\#

I

didn't

want

to

love

her

but

she

came

like

the

wind

no

matter

how

perfect

your

vision

no

one

will

ever

see

the

wind

coming

\#

some midnights

I stand outside

watching the sky

for shooting stars

not to make a wish

but to pay homage

for it stayed

as long as it could

just as love does

it stays

as long as it could

love never leaves

because it wants to

it leaves because

it has to

forever's are built

not wished for

eternity is work

continually

in process

progress

is discovered

in the not

giving up part

stars will remain

the perfect

example

of light

what if there were no titles

into darkness

of giving all

with no expectations

I have heard

some will take back

their all

but has learned

as stars

teach us

all is not capable

of being retrieved

once given

it's the light

in our eyes

the sky's

in our sockets

reminding me

of heaven

and how

the last flash

of a shooting star

was never meant

to be used

for wishing

but to show us

how bright

forever

will glow

when it leaves

#

I've kept all the pieces of dreams

broken accidentally or on purpose

no one arrives on this earth

with knowledge of how

to hold a dream properly

without breaking an edge or corner

without snapping it clean in two

I have broken many myself

prefer to claim it accidental

wanted to see what I was made of

in the beginning we are so fragile

could shatter at first doubt

I keep filling empty pages

with hopes and wishes

most will mistake for a poem

some may read as a prayer

either way I am sending to them heaven

in the slightest case they turn out to be both

I hear hope is for sale

it cost too much, you can't barter for it

and can't do much with it

unless you decide to put in the pain

only then will hope become a dream

and dreams can become your purpose

if you run fast enough

with it strapped to your chest

I think I read somewhere

about the winds of change

what if there were no titles

stated as if you didn't know

change was coming

were not aware

it was probably needed

change is what

you do for yourself

when you need some better

to combat some worse

when you know 911

is the number to call

when you break yourself

cause help ain't coming

you have to find belief

in the healing powers

of love - in loving yourself

in letting go

you can find strength

in possibility, in faith

in walking, in running

you can't arrive to any

destination or desired location

until you begin to move

be sure to move on purpose

run toward purpose

hold on to dreams and never let go

as sure as the sun will shine tomorrow

help isn't on its way - help ain't coming

it has always been

you against you

\#

some days it is hard to see past sun

not the burst of rays or glares

bright enough to catch you off guard

it's the fact I am still here

basking in its light

no one will tell you

you won't receive a message of confirmation

my bones know there is so much more

I am destined to get done

I hear the constant cheers for the underdog

you can hear the rally cry for those in last place

legs churning as if running left miles ago

I catch a listen to the wind

voices of friends tangled in the breeze

I would never attach sound to anyone specific

it seems there are those angry

I am still here turning impossible's

into about to happen

I know how it feels

when you think those on your side

are actually on your side

or anchored in complete opposition

I got mission plans from heaven

with no instructions on how to accomplish

got more fight in me than the battle requires

if life is test of wills or simply built of obstacles

I must be living two of them at once

some days sliding downhill

what if there were no titles

will feel the same as climbing up

will be harder than the constant

tug of war with destiny

I know fate hates to see me coming

got too many questions to let him pass

with a multitude of answers

he has yet to formulate questions for

this writing thing is real

I don't know where

these thoughts come from

or how they arrive so fast

I will capture a glimpse of a thought

see purpose in a shadow or cloud

everyone is different

not visible to human eyes

I always feel the need to apologize

to those I shared I love you's with

I know all, forever, always and eternity

are the most frequently used words

when hearts are involved

most fail to test the all on themselves

I know how heavy my all is

but wasn't aware it could be a burden

when placed on someone else's shoulders

I greet the sun every day

with a loud good morning

not that all mornings start out good

there is something in the way

a sudden burst of new rays makes you feel

there are so many possibilities

appearing in new light

you could not discover

in the midst of darkness

I plan each day to be my best

not for sure how many mountains

or trails will clutter my path

but there is something in the sun

letting me know everything is possible

even when you lose everything

you thought you

paid enough to possess

even when your follow through

doesn't have the adequate through

you were sure you placed in it

I am darkness in the light

a shadow caressing a new day

knowing how to squeeze

every piece of promise

out of this one may take

more than twenty four hours

there is no such thing as a tomorrow

when it gets here we label it now

all we will ever have is now

this sun, these rays

a bright glare of possibles

we must seize the most out of

before the moon appears

fooling us - trying to make us

what if there were no titles

think rest is needed

how can you rest

when you're still fighting time

for some more right now

some more sun

there are so many possibilities

appearing in light

you could never discover

entrapped in darkness

and this right now

is the best opportunity

to test your all on yourself

there are no scales

or ways to balance

what you've given

against what you think

you've received

stop saying the best is yet to come

use this sun and this right now

to drag your best

from its hiding place

there are no such things

as tomorrows

just the appearance

of a new today

if you are blessed

to bask in the rays

in the glare and sun

of the next right now

\#

there are

lessons in lonely

all of us have them

unaware we are equipped

for no one told us

they were keepable

we didn't know

they were lessons

I watch myself

be whole and half

in the same moment

the whole part moving on

the half of me stands still

reaching back

waiting for someone

who will never know

you are waiting

expecting them to remember

I gave my word

I would be here until then

whenever then happens to be

they must've forgotten

sometimes words

are lost in translation

losing their meaning

when love takes flight

it's really hard to gauge

when love takes flight

what if there were no titles

we never knew love had wings

there are lessons in lonely

you can only find in lonely

not the lonely when left alone

lessons lie in that other lonely

the one where you found yourself

dusted off your brokenness

patch the visible holes

cleaned off your pride

put it back exactly where

you thought it was originally

no one knows where pride goes

when you discover

it has been missing

I discovered I had been missing

it only happens when you escape

when you leave the lonely

you placed yourself in

you will find there is always

that other lonely

you will hear things of you

real words from friends

making you not like you

the same way

and reason they stopped

you will check your pulse

your driver's license

your pockets wishing you kept

remnants to remember you by

here is the good part

you are still here

knowing you are here

joining the whole and the half

will not make you whole again

it will help you to remember

there are lessons

in lonely

that are lessons

that are keepable

keep them close

not for keepsakes

you will require them

when there is no more

lonely to remember

when the unexpected happens

when they reach for you

thinking half of you

must still be waiting

the one thing you must know

is it is easy to mistake

the pain in your palms

for stickiness of love

you will find

you are closely attached

to the next lonely you meet

two lonely's can be love

but only if they've

learned their lessons

\#

I keep trying

not to remember

nights heaven won't forget

how I stroked you with fingers

until your clothes fell off

how I spoke in silence to your body

until it responded in convulsions

I have the skills of a doctor

the hands of a surgeon

and the tongue - well a tongue

you said should be declared

a weapon of ecstasy revisited

I hear how your legs shake

during our hello's

I see how your back bends

long before we approach goodbye

and your hips sway from side to side

as we speak of today's weather

your body knows my voice

you sweat the instant

I touch your arm

your skin and I

are call and response

it calls me - I respond

I had a hand in creating

that rhythm you walk with

I must have licked you a symphony

explained to your clitoris

this is how you dance

my tongue

will be the music

you scream to

I am sure heaven

will never forget

as I try my best

not to remember

how light your legs

are on my shoulders

how they continue

to squeeze my waist

as you demand they stop

your body replies

in a cadence

more mine than yours

you only watched

movies about this

we should make

movies about this

we may have

exchanged bodies

in the exchange

it's Friday could be

make a movie night

or maybe you need

me to bring

my orchestra of a tongue

and lick you a symphony

\#

I am in love with clouds

especially those wearing

tints of grey - they do me good

we've been romancing

and dancing for years

there is something magical

when the first drops of rain

lands gently on your face

I love the rain

maybe that's why

so many cultures

ask it to arrive in dances

I have my own rain dance

although it doesn't always work

it frees my soul

feels good to these feet

life keeps testing the run in

testing if they could balance

themselves on uneven problems

on the beast of trials

too big to handle alone

knowing they must be

handled alone

I am good with lonely

with clouds dancing as I do

in the fresh downpour

of the welcomed rain

I remember the first time

I sat in the park

bottle of wine, two glasses

a bench to rest my weary

and watch the scamper

of those not knowing

the dance of rain

not aware of its

cleansing properties

moments like this

are what life is for

why we are given days

of sun, of cold, of rain

each possessing qualities

for love to be shared

I find the most intimate

moments in wet clothes

in thinking your wet

is from thoughts of the

dance we do

in the closed door practice

of welcoming rain

we make happen

I was told once

I move as lightning

it is the rain dances

making other dances look as if

you're attempting to create a downpour

I will make you downpour

every time we dance - our dance of rain

what if there were no titles

\#

if in this moment

I begin to

thank my mother

for all of the gifts of love

I have been blessed with

it would take

volumes of pages

circles of sages

just to start

I would have to surgically

remove my heart

dissect each part

trace the ventricles and veins

as proof to the pain

I have managed

to stand true

I can't take credit

just because I said it

I give credit where credit is due

and mama believe me

I owe all of me to you

you are an extension

of everything I will ever do

and this love I've learned

I learned from you

love you much more

than this dance of words

could ever prove

\#

I used to love writing

loved the sound and rhythm

of fine point pens

sliding smoothly across pages

until it begin to feel

as if I was carving words

and thoughts with fingers

teeth and bones

there was too much me

displayed for viewing

everything I've written

can be placed back

into this body

in the exact spot

it was removed from

nothing is easy

at first glance

you will not hear

your own footsteps

will not see you go

won't be aware

of the distance

you will just arrive

in a strange place

as familiar as the left side

of your right foot

wearing a spectacular

look of wonder

what if there were no titles

amazed you didn't feel

the journey

love is not a

good Samaritan

it will trip you

push you down

and refuse to

help you to your feet

will not point you

in the direction of home

love doesn't care

if your balance

has been stolen

it will only leave you

with one choice

loving is not

a choice you make

it will be made for you

before you know it

you would believe

your heart possessed fingers

or a long arm with strong muscles

the way it snatched your attention

the way it ripped your emotions

from the places

you didn't know emotions lived

late is thinking you're early

thinking you have time to change

to put on your best smile

to make yourself

presentable

offering likes instead

of love you's

late is attempting

to use human hands

to catch yourself

while falling

writing was always

my comfort zone

until it begin

revealing my secrets

I hid them so well

my heart had forgotten

how to read them

you will never know

who is waiting

to steal your precious

to raid the treasure

of your kisses

you will not

hear them coming

they will simply

arrive at your lips

I still love writing

still enjoy the music

of fine tipped pens

on blank sheets of miracles

I recently arrived

what if there were no titles

at a point

of understanding

too late to know

too far gone to be

any good for myself

don't know how

I got here

or why waiting

brings smiles

I guess love

makes herself new

every time she finds me

here chest open, mouth wide

arms extended, eyes wishing

need brings more pain than wanting

I didn't write of needing

it showed up out of nowhere

there are bones in my pen

love will have you

breathing life

performing CPR

on every tomorrow

before it arrives

love has the perfect ability

to make herself new

each time she finds me

needing, waiting, wishing

writing in rhythm

amazed of the journey

\#

when there

is only dirt

no yellow brick road

when you knew

at the very start

the wizard was a lie

when you are aware

tornados

when applicable

to dreams

can be defined

as doubt

bundled with fear

and fear has nothing

to do with rain

or storms

and you can be certain

storms are coming

when you order

the number of books

you knew

you didn't have

the funds

in your account

to remit

the amount required

when you run blindly

through the forest

what if there were no titles

believing the trees

will move

open a path - guide you

when you leap

as far as possible

from the top

of the mountain

knowing the bridge

is invisible

and strong enough

to bare your weight

when you search

the night sky

for shooting stars

not to make a wish

but to pay homage

it stayed as long as it could

you are no longer a dream

chaser or catcher

you build them from scratch

believing has nothing

to do with thinking it is so

but has everything to do with

knowing the manifestation

of necessary will follow you

wherever you lead

faith is never blind

it is the guidance system

of dreamers who refuse to sleep

#

every day

I try and wish

a little harder

close my eyes

a little tighter

hoping

the little boy

in me

would remember

how it felt

to be a dream

I think that's when

I believed in wishes

believed love

conquers all

believed in

fairytales

love at first sight

and magic

it's hard

not to believe

you are magic

you are

the fairytale

I wrote

wishing

I would hope

you could meet

what if there were no titles

the little boy

in me

he is

the biggest doubter

and needs to see you

to view how

love looks close up

I stopped wishing

when you got here

started back wishing

praying you would stay

I even pray

in wishes now

while holding hands

with the little boy in me

waiting

hoping to see you

in order to

believe again

and know

this is

you are

wishable

wearing promise

in smiles

knowing

you are

what love

looks like

\#

I wrote a poem every day

hiding in it a warning

change was on its way

heard it in my pen

saw it in the clouds

listened as the moon

whispered softly

to the coming day

the sun shouted

change is coming

each morning upon arrival

either knowing or thinking

others would take note

or take heed only to find

change was here already

most payed no attention

spans were too short

many would rather

bask in the pain

waddle uncontrollably

in yesterday's misery

most missed the message

because the poems

were too long

or maybe

used all of the caring

available on forgettables

and forget me soons

\#

the last time

or was it the first

maybe it was each time it happened

I can only remember how wet

how drenched emotions

will leave you

sometimes floods will rush in

you won't expect or know how

to stop the rain

or your eyes from leaking

I think it was the last time

or maybe the first

could it be some hearts

practice leaving

I know most people wish to stay

I don't blame the person

it is never their fault

I blame love

love comes with so much expectation

with so many embraces and kisses

love only knows love

it doesn't know people

doesn't understand its place

it has no real place we can understand

I think it wants to stay when it gets here

it doesn't want to leave

most will believe they created it

grew it from lust

watched it blossomed
from overwhelming want
but love only knows love
it doesn't understand games
most people play games with love
and wonder why it can't stay
never again will I blame a person
for inconstancies for wanting things
to only be the way
they want things to be
I blame love
for arriving all wrapped in glory
for shining in the darkest of times
bringing an abundance of smiles
we will forget
how to smile on our own
will believe
we smile because of love
but love doesn't know smiling
doesn't know happy
can't comprehend
why we depend on it so
love only knows love
I wish someone had taught me
to learn love from walking
from moving - from the motion
we find in laughing - in crying
I am sure love wants to stay
if we make it comfortable enough

what if there were no titles

if we explain

sometimes pain

will come but doesn't last long

hurt is more a part

of this human condition

we didn't learn to avoid

we are obligated to confront

even when avoidable

love doesn't know hurt

can't understand pain

love only knows love

and we are still

waiting to meet it

for the first time

or maybe the last

I know I am ready

to teach love to stay

to ask it what it wants

I don't know

love's language

the one thing I know

is love only knows love

it doesn't know people

or places or yesterday's

it doesn't know leaving

I am sure love

only knows love

and it really wants

to stay

\#

I stood there silent as Angels

bombarded me with questions

I knew God was somewhere watching

I had no choice but to answer

what color?

dark tan but I call it black

what type of eyes?

I need to see clear to the soul... so brown

how tall?

not a threating height... six feet even

what tongue?

I would prefer a language

stolen like my people

pieced together to leave room

for creating new words

what gender?

make me man of African descent

I want to know how struggle feels

between my teeth and gums

hair? let it be nappy... like Jesus

I know they will never understand

why locs formed from a few strands

of hair would represent any group

of people in unity

job?

leave that open

I want to try my hand at a few

job?

what if there were no titles

I would love

to speak your word

your truth, why don't you place

your tongue on mine

and make me a poet

a truth sayer of life

job?

give me the hands of those

unable to speak for themselves

fingers untiring, let me paint

in metaphoric colors

in complete sentences

fill my heart with ink

let it runneth over

cover my skin in patience

my eyes in caring

my arms in warmth

for those wanting out of the cold

make me an empty vessel

an empty cup let be filled

with the joys of life

if not a poet then give me

a new name, teacher, wordartist,

philosopher, prophet, tiller of souls

planter of promise,

a soldier of knowledge

truthfully God

I would be most honored

if you would make me a POET

Bonus Verses

This section of words were added to include poems performed, written for performance and those I wanted to include for the next book may not be one containing Poetry.

Thank you for reading

-ajh-

what if there were no titles

These poems would have never found their way in any book, I thought including them would offer a more indebt view of the movement of my pen. Thank you for reading. Your comments are appreciated... send your thoughts to poetajhouston@gmail.com

Table of Additional Content...

Breathe	357
Full Moon	359
One More Sun	362
No More Lyrics	365
This Is The Last Time I Fix Broken (1)	368
Thoughts, Words and Dreams	370
Three Things You Must Do When Falling From Heaven	374
Locs	378
Mirrors	381
Dreams	384
I Learned to Say Your Name In My Sleep	387
Note To Self	390
The Word	393
Writing 101	396
In Slumber	499
My Life In Rhythm	402
Lost	405
The Moon	409
Support The Artist	413
Acknowledgements	414
About The Author	415
Contact Information	416

Thank you for the opportunity to present, these etchings, a painting of moments as seen through my pen.

Breathe

good morning Allah, today's prayer will be brief

thank You for breath... ase' – ase'

in quiet moments I've become the explorer of me

breathe

to the one who took residence in the twist of my locs

before I knew there was room for you to stay

breathe

it must have been a month or so after you left

I noticed

ever so often my chest would skip a breath

unbeknownst to any bystander's

just the in part, the outs are forever automatic

breathe

there is a case of memories

stashed in the back of my heart

so intricate apart of my existence

I will never forget, even the secrets

of my secrets have secrets

you've left me no choice

but to hide from myself

afraid of the lovemares revealed when I sleep

the human body must be the eighth sense

storing unnoticeable breaths for safe keeping

to offer in place of the I love you's

breathe

knowing there has to be something better than all

something worth more than hugs and touching

a benevolent offering - a sacrificing of flesh

what if there were no titles

a permanent blemish on my records in the halls of forever

my knees have become those of a beggar

eyes photoshop your face on every woman I pass

if you want to know of my recent discoveries

my fingerprints are perfect replicas of the cells on your skin

they miss you more than I

imagine... if heaven can be measured in bites and slices

it would taste just like you

there is this space between loving and living

requiring a bridge to cross over

I'm stuck on the wrong side

some days it becomes too hard to bare

too impossible to draw you in sentences on pages

too loud the thoughts as silence gives way to tears

as my chest skips a breath

breathe

there are bends in the bows of these arms

a curvature in the center of my chest

indentations in the corners of my smile

where you are the perfect fit

breathe

I had hoped to bundle these breaths I've been saving

to conceal in the wind - to blend in the blaze of the sun

to disguise in the clouds - as tears in the rain

a cloak in the darkness - to bury in the trees

to live in a song - to gift in the small of your back

just in case you ever noticed - you skipped a breath too

every one of these I've stored - I'm saving for you

breathe

Full Moon

I must have been born during a storm

or birthed underneath a lightning rod

I have a fondness for dark clouds

gathering at the break of day

a great adoration for the sudden downpour

of the tears of angels

everything I've ever needed to say

forms a hurricane my lips cannot control the passing of

I treat thunder as applause

for my inability to find comfort in the giving of all

but all is the only item I have to give since the beginning

before the first wind of the first storm

I met you under a full moon - I am sure of it now

the waves in my body gravitated to you

as though you were made of shore

the rumblings of the heavens

was how I was told to greet you

it was foretold in the stars

written on the edges of oceans

by the footprints of the most high

storms only last for days

all can endure a total

of three life cycles of human existence

our hearts stood eye to eye - beat to beat

each pulse moved at the exact moment

the sun became the moons shadow

I held you like a lunar eclipse

the ones you shield your pupils from

what if there were no titles

the kind scientists say

the slightest gaze

would render you blind

we are a perfect mixture

of star dust and comets

a sort of multicolored rubik's cube

twisting and turning to line up

the noticeable seams remaining

when our undoctored hands

attempt to repair or mend

our own fractured hearts

we are torn retinas and swollen tongues

unable to see or say what matters most

at a time when most things matter

we are easy bake oven angerturnovers

assorted cupcakes topped with hurt feelings

a cosmic array of patience would be

what the surgeon general ordered

but we are too skilled at subversion

of manipulating our attire for anyone to notice

our brokenness or witness our flaws

we are shooting star memories

the lost lines of our life story

most believe a fairytale to great to be forgotten

the folklores sung by wishful bystanders

we are the scribes typing our misfortune

carving the history of loves battle

into open skies for the clouds to share

we are the words with breath

that will live longer

than this skin on loan

to cover our bones

so easily scarred

love has no shelf life

it cannot be removed or destroyed

I met you under a full moon

barely visible through darkened clouds

I am the god child of tsunamis

with an asteroid for a tongue

you are butterfly beautiful

rainbow to my storm

a flash of brilliance, a rising Phoenix

the rendered glory of my imagination

answers to questions I was too afraid to ask

I should have listened to scientists

and never looked into your soul

I met you under a full moon

I am sure of it now

you can never learn the secrets of storms

unless you're taught to listen closely

using fingers as a guide

to circle each moment

meant to be cherished

I gather strength from rain

from tears angels send to shroud my sadness

I am the son of storms

stolen whispers hidden in thunder

and I love, by every drop of rain that falls

what if there were no titles

One More Sun

I must've been around eleven

when my favorite aunt died

in an automobile accident

it was the first time I experienced

something I will never be able to explain

she came to visit me right after it happened

I could see her, arms outstretched

the usual great hug she gave only me

made my other siblings jealous

but this time, that one night

she looked different

eyes were not happy or sad

but were trying to glare a good bye

all I could do was scream

from the top of the bunk bed

startled the whole house

I remember the look on my father's face

that turn of lip pissed don't equate

only hours before the alarm was set

I told everyone what I experienced

it was her, beautiful smile the same

eyes saying good bye

It had to be about three a.m.

at four a.m. barely an hour past screams

the phone rang - more screams followed

my father was given the news

not that I knew but I knew something

at eleven eyes are hard to discern

I remember asking God

for one more Sun

get her home

she was my favorite

and I had lots of favorite aunts

but she used to sit with me

tell me about my now then

told me how smart I was

how I was different from the rest

she knew then

I needed her

she could never leave

without saying good bye

even if eleven year olds

didn't know or understand

the language of eyes

given one more sun

she would have told me

more of my now then

she gave me hugs that lasted

her voice faint but still clear

still rings of love

just one more sun

I would ask all the questions

I ever need to know

would ask why love hurts

why loving leaves no scars

just so much pain

I would ask her why I was different

what if there were no titles

ask if she knew words of hers

would remain and escape daily

through these hands

she taught to patty cake

if she was aware

25 hotdogs in one day

wouldn't make me fat

as my cousins were claiming

with one more sun

I would tell her I love her

she is my favorite

I believe she knew

my tomorrows yesterday

she knew her goodbye

would be too soon

for a boy eleven to understand

what good bye meant

God... if we had one more sun

I would ask her how to love

how to wrap it so tightly

it would never want to leave

never offer silence or good bye's

in the language of eyes

if I had just one more sun

I would hold her from now to then

with one of those special hugs

she only gave me

made my siblings jealous

all I need... is one more sun

No More Lyrics

I have been a metaphor

since I was three years old

when my mother taught me to read

when I believed a cat could wear a hat

things could become twins, fish could talk

and eggs could possibly have tints of green

my mother told me I could speak things into being

long before I read it for myself

in the bible she carried by her side

more than she carried her purse

I wish I could write you a poem

that didn't sound like it had been edited

I write edited, read too much, memory is too good

thesaurus in my throat, dictionary lives in my fingers

my father will tell you if he could

broken English skipped a generation

I wanted to write a poem you would like

 that sounded how you listen

I remember how you listen, memory is too good

to tell you how good memory is

I see the words your hands move to

I could write like you - I used to write like you

I need to write like you, or rather like you listen

so your ears can hear my meaning

I am no way implying you don't understand me

fact is... you don't want your friends to know you understand me

your friends control the way your tongue moves

tells you what to bob your head to

what if there were no titles

I truly understand some circles

are hard to break

when you've all spent time broken

there is a complicated process

delivering a blank canvas to an empty mind

attempting to fill it with thoughts said mind didn't create

I wrote simple when I was four

on brown paper bags

while shopping with my mother at the store

wrote on strips of paper at the laundry

passed them to her with head down

writing and sharing what is written

has always been a humbling experience

she would quickly scan the contents

then place them in the bible she carried by her side

more than she carried her purse

I don't write because I want to, or because I have to

I write because God gave me no other options

hid poems in my socks, replaced the food in my lunch

with new thoughts, new verses to create

I've been a metaphor every since I was three

I have always been my daddy's middle child

with two middle fingers - I never had to use

I knew your matters didn't matter

had no revelation in my process of living

couldn't understand why you think they would

words only matter when they are torn

ripped away leaving scars as memory

I want to give you words your mind

can use for nourishment later

sit them by your bedside

take your time

words don't know rush

and can only live

when they have been released

I only write because my mother told me

I could speak things into being

told me my voice

sounded kind of like... love

God made my fingers to fit pens perfectly

heaven told me to write

I want to write like you

I don't listen to the music you listen to

or watch the movies you watch

I used to, I can only write like me

I don't want you to write like me

I need you to write like you

only that better you

I mean - with more you in it

more true in it

I mean - I want you to write

as you would write

if you hadn't heard those words

from other poets

you keep trying to write like

my mother would tell you too

you possess a certain tone in your voice

that sounds kind of... kind of like... love

what if there were no titles

This Is The Last Time I Fix Broken (1)

my grandmother taught me

falling is going to happen

dust yourself off

scars will heal

you will remember

the hardest falls forever

sometimes you will break yourself

there will be moments

of discontent, of sorrow

nothing will ever be

as good as you want

or as bad as you claim

you will learn to embellish

lie - to make believe

sympathy is for those

too weak to bare the burdens

life has given them to cherish - to carry

sometimes you will break yourself

sometimes love crashes

goes up in flames

some relationships

will smash and grab

the best parts of you

broken is just what it is - broken

as long as all the pieces remain

you can fix your brokenness

no one will tell you

when your heart is missing

when the lids of your eyes

can't stop the running of oceans

this is the last time I fix broken

the last time I will use these hands

to remanufacture a damn

love leaks too much

to build a new seal

securing the space

the exit, the opening

my missing rib tends to let

distracting smiles steal my heart through

where yesterday's arrive late

with enough strength bend the curve

in the corners of my lips downwards

where pain forms arthritic clinches

this is the last time I fix broken

the last time I believe

these legs won't give out

falling is going to happen

there are times I may break myself

may crack under the pressure

real all is too heavy to carry by yourself

It takes two to bare the weight of forever

tomorrow's come with the surprise

of its own circumstance

there will be days

you empty the ocean

through the outlets

of the corners of your eyes

what if there were no titles

Thoughts, Words and Dreams

here at Thoughts, Words and Dreams
we specialize in the creative process
analyzing your output to equal your input
or rather creating a better method of input
to make your output better
have you experienced quit in your pen
a slow progression of thoughts
have your hands refused
to pick up your favorite writing utensil
did someone recently lie to you
tell you there is such a thing
as writers block? well that's bullshhh
there is only writers stop
you can't write what's next
if you fail to address your now
have you attended a workshop
that didn't work
left you with only time to shop
for new work
the wait is over
you have arrived at your destination
here at Thoughts, Words and Dreams
we do not... I repeat do not
perform creative writing workshops
we created the Psychology of Writing Institute
to help you understand why write
if you do not understand why you write
how will you ever be able write your why

we do life sessions to help you discover
the power in the discovery of you
you are creative already
we will teach your fingers
they also have ears
and can listen to that little voice
you didn't know was your voice
there are more you's in you
than you have agreed to let out
we will unlock the inside door
to your inside self
so outside self and inside self
will finally be properly introduced
I'm Dreams - I'm Words – I'm Thoughts
hey… hey… that's not the right order
ok… ok… I'm Thoughts - I'm Words - I'm Dreams
here at Thoughts, Words and Dreams
we don't think outside the box
we've been aware for years
there was never a f ing box
there are no borders on pages
those lines are where you place
the extra truth
no one told you were truths
stop letting others tell you
what they think you should know
tell yourself what you know you know
here at Thoughts, Words and Dreams
we teach you how to think like you

what if there were no titles

how to write like you

we will prove

your words are worth

their weight in galaxies

when they are actually

your words

have you received

the same writing prompt

at the last eight

workshops you attended

did they have

the same diatribe

same script

same exact words

as the last instructors did?

trying to show how poetry

can be an essay - short story

children's book - stage play

but only if you

keep telling yourself it is

that's bullshhh

were you aware each human

was created with four eyes

two eyes to see the human in you

two eyes to expand

the human out of you

were you aware gravity

is here to help you stay

but not to keep you here

your pen is weightless

imagine there is no pen

just a miracle appearing in ink

now... cut out that bullShhh

and write a miracle

at Thoughts, Words and Dreams

we place emphasis on better

better you

better thoughts

better writing

better! yea better!

(last response slower) better!

bullshhh, is bullshhh

no matter how you

shovel it - write it - perform it

call us at 1- 800 – A Betta U

follow us

on Instagram

& twitter

like us on facebook

hash tag no mo bullshhh

hash tag write a miracle

hash tag we got yo pen hostage

what the hell?

here at Thoughts, Words and Dreams

we can fix

your broken, lost - forgotten

hash tag No Mo Bullshhh

contact us at 1 – 800- A Betta U

what if there were no titles

Three Things You Must Do When Falling From Heaven

there is an explanation for everything

even the things there are no explanations for

that's a little gem an angel gifted me

at least I thought she was

she tasted of seraphim

the first thing to remember

applicable to all facets of life

always, always... I mean always

keep pen and paper with you at all times

a fact I understood a bit late

for I should've written everything down

no one plans or ever expects

to fall from heaven

until you're wide eyed and screaming

in the middle of your decent

heaven is a long way from silence to thump

beware of wings... or any woman

with remnants of feathers in her hair

it's the smile, the star dust on her lips

yielding the capacity to catch you off guard

oh yea! always keep your guard

where it is easily retrievable

there are few things worse

than being caught dancing or dining

while leaving your guard at home

and no one will ever tell you what they are

innocence is a nuclear device

wrapped in swaddling clothes

with it's face covered up

I learned this the hard way

practice, practice, practice

you must practice landing

before you begin to believe

there is a sky

before you faith base

your fairytales into existence

before you purposefully

infect your dreams with promise

this will become

the most valuable tool

in your arsenal

impossible

is waiting to acquire a technique

after you've been made aware

such a technique or skill

may someday be required

none of us are masters

of the pop quiz or listening

understand most stars

are too far off

to be of consequence

or of any significance

when shooting or falling

you will never hear it's scream

or see first hand

the lesson

abrupt stops has to teach us

what if there were no titles

remember... always yell!
the whispering voices of angels
are as intoxicating as coal dust from diamonds
the melody will get you got
laugh! laughing may someday be
as valuable as landing
learn to laugh at yourself
there will be times skill and technique
will fail and laughter will be the only thing
you have to help you land safely
halos are not night lamps
as bright as they are
they don't glow in the dark
love is a mountain draped in a parachute
It cannot fly no matter how you center it
or how deep you bury it
underneath an angels breast
our fingers are faulty
they will never be able
to hold anything as tight
or as long as we thought they could
do not be fearful of letting go
do not listen for your name to be called
or spoken - or whispered
or mentioned in your presence
for it will be dark, cold,
swollen, dismembered and bloody
scrapped from the tongues
of friends and loved ones

who tossed it about so many times

it will no longer sound caressed

and reverenced as it did some days ago

hold your head high

let them see the you they knew

before you became the person

someone else's pain painted

a couple of shades darker

rings around your eyes

a touch of horn showing

when you turn your head to the left

never forget in this America

black men in all historical records

were disemboweled, gutted

and hung - name first

your character is what they can't destroy

you will have to brace it for support

too many knives in back

will weigh heavy on your soul

laugh! laugh out loud

when you finally discover

there will be no safe place to land

only hands that push

that rip not catch

you will be fine

when falling from heaven

remember, most people fail to believe

in its existence anyway

you... you will be fine

what if there were no titles

LOCs (team Piece with Brentom (Chuck Jackson)

the last time I went to the barbershop

when my turn came - he looked at me

before he could ask - I said

AJ - mustache trim

Chuck - edge up

That too

AJ - I found myself sitting in front of a poster

Chuck - with a myriad of heads accompanied by numbers

he said... pick one... **it's Saturday**... there is a long line behind you

AJ - bald fade, **Chuck** - mohawk, **AJ** - dark taper – **Chuck** the caesar

AJ I have always wondered
Chuck when they were captured and chained

did they know their heads would displayed
and used as styles for others to mimic?

AJ - you can learn everything in the barbershop

politrics, AJ - how to pick up women

Chuck - they have the best movie reviews

the barber asked me the usual questions

AJ - but when he asked why locs?

Chuck - everyone stopped to listen

I paused... not that I didn't expect the question

I was completely aware none of them were ready for the answer

AJ - sometimes you have to start at the beginning

Chuck - not everyone will agree but as historical records go

Samson had seven - not saying I'm a nasserite

AJ - could be could be not, **Chuck - w**ho's to say

and sometimes you have to start with revolution

Jamaican Maroons:

Chuck - the first documented community of escaped slaves in the Caribbean

often referred to by their ex-masters **as having dreadful locs**

funny how those always seem to be linked

AJ - freedom, community, **Chuck -** government, ownership

locks... locs... **I mean locs**

what's sad is most people think it's a fad

AJ - myspace, **Chuck -** Vanilla Ice, **AJ -** selfies, **Chuck -** Macklemore

AJ - skinny jeans, **Chuck -** Iggy Azalea

because one loc is a collection of many strains

Chuck - and community is made of free women and free men

AJ - embracing the natural state of things, fighting to untwist the chains they were given

Chuck - perms, **AJ -** locs, **Chuck -** weaves

AJ - locs, **Chuck -** extensions, **AJ -** locs

corporations claim to embrace diversity

police will testify   Chuck - this was a DUI

AJ - driving while under the influence

Chuck - not a DWL, **AJ -** driving while locked

others find anger when they see the history in our - locs

they can still see the splinters from slave ships

shredded pieces of rope

drenched in the tears of those sold on auction blocks

these are the images locked into my locs

but I've found borrowed tongues trying to build a nation

what if there were no titles

out of positive thoughts in our locs

Chuck - I found kindred spirits in the faith of our locs

King Seti the first, father of Ramses the second

Chuck - Jon Michele Basquiat

AJ - Jesus the Nasserite

pardon Assata

free Mumia

sing 'Redemption Song'

wear your hair as our ancestors did

holy, proud and strong

to our surprise, no one in the barbershop was talking

no politricks

Chuck - no homemade soul food plates

AJ - no bootleg dvd's to sale

Chuck - even the women held their sons a little closer

AJ - and the men gazed at that cage of slaves on the wall

I told them ...

Chuck - hurry up

its Saturday

AJ - pick one

there is a long line of slaves behind you

but

I

don't

do

locks!!!

Mirrors

there is a mirror

on the other side of the mirror

a reflection reflecting your reflections

you probably aren't aware of

how you see yourself seeing yourself

a reverse view - a hidden you

we hide the best of us, not sure if we are ready

its the reason we talk to ourselves

play absent and not hear the answer

rest assured we do answer every time

I remember the first time, I saw me seeing me

too afraid to join the conversation

an interbody experience, most will not participate

for fear of understanding the complications

of your inside self not following protocols

set into law by your outside self

using only ten percent of your brain

doesn't offer enough amperage

to be the president of your own purpose

the official conductor in your concert of dreams

I would tell you how it went

the moment I discovered these things were true

but unbelievers usually stop listening

failing to read any further than the first couple of lines

any attempt to order these fingers to cease

will not reach the control center

as usual they just keep typing

you will require a crossing guard

what if there were no titles

thoughts seldom notice stop signs

when on a mission to completion

will not yield the right of way

shocked... is you acting surprised

when you declare some of your own pursuits

futile - not worth the five watts of power

your brain used to create them

I will always embrace every reflection

even those looking slightly unfamiliar

it must have been a me in an earlier time

or will become me at a later date

I am not for sure how this works, if the sign in sheet is blank

I won't be able to tell you which me you spoke to

or make clear the me you are presently speaking with

sometimes some of the me's don't attend all the meetings

will openly protest the gatherings, or shows up

a day late demanding to read the minutes

the secretary me is too slow, can't keep up

with the arguments - don't feel comfortable with conflict

but there will be no resolve without it

I am finding watching me watch me

takes years of adjustments

if you want to know how others see you

study first how you see yourself

there will be things you do, you won't agree with

and things you would like to change

you need to attend or call a meeting

to see if all the you's will vote I to

the body is a democracy, the majority rules

even in your own frame

sometimes you will not appoint you president

and may be asked to leave the premises

receive a full escort out of your mind

it happened to me before, but I knew I needed me too

couldn't give up that easy, do not fear your reflection

your rejection of you will be common place

relish in the fact there has been a lot of you's

over the span of time you'd had breath

there will be days, happy will greet you

before your eyes open, or tears will awaken you

without you knowing why

life is a much more experienced teacher

than we will ever be at studenting

learn everything you can about yourself

even things you wish you didn't know

wishing some of those you's would've kept hidden in the vault

no one told this you the combination to

the next time you look in the mirror, be quick about it

before you discover you are not as pretty

or as handsome as you told yourself yesterday

heaven may have painted more gray

added a few extra pounds to the structure

than you remember asking for

you will arrive at places, you never asked to be

you will be there for a reason

ask yourself why - but this time

pay attention, wait for the answer

rest assured... we do answer every time

what if there were no titles

Dreams

I have been bouncing my dreams

through this cosmos

through star systems

no one has noticed yet

dreams don't care where they come from

don't care where they go

they need us more than we need them

we only exist because they exist

without them we be stumbling about

wondering where going be

and where we be going

dreams were here before us

before earth, before sound

before let there be, it was the reason

for let there be

dreams been sitting here - waiting

waiting on us to wake up and find them

we keep finding them thinking

them just dreams - my dreams be bigger

but these be big dreams, giant dreams

these be them let there be dreams

them why there is light dreams

I found one of them small dreams

when I was small - this dream grew with me

this is that same dream, it grow bigger than life

I can't hold this dream

got to give parts of this dream away

you gon learn

your dreams will stop you from dreaming
until you treat your first dream right
until you understand
dreams don't come in bunches
unless you grow them in bushels
and buckets watered with tears
I cried over these a long time
to get them to this size
these be bushels of big dreams
I growed from that mustard seed
of a dream
I got books filled with dreams
I been growing
them eyes of friends
don't read them dreams
I guess they be too big to read
but you can't get no new dreams
till you grow them old dreams
you had when you were small
you don growed but your dreams still young
I got dreams for sale, I got dreams for sale
and these be your dreams
you just don't remember what they look like
you all growed up, and these be still small
me and my dreams started out gospel sanging
we be hallelujahing - and shouting
then we rapped - and r & b'd a little
then we jazzed and grooved and trumpeted
then we poeted - yea poeted

what if there were no titles

we been poeting for a while

got to take them in this bag with me

you can't leave your dreams nowhere

cause your dreams will leave you

will forget what you look like

I got dreams for sale

and these be your dreams

I got new dreams on they way back

my dreams been space walking

ain't enough space on this here planet

for my dreams - I got them big dreams

growed up from small dreams

them walking on water kind of dreams

them got up three days later kind of dreams

them don't need wings to fly dreams

them dreams slaves seen when walking with truth

I got freedom dreams

I got dreams that be running free

I got dreams with they own feet

these be awesome dreams, I got mountain dreams

them carry me away dreams

them bigger than me dreams

I just need to know

when you gon go back over yonder

up there, to yo mothers house

and get you dreams - I got dreams for sale

I got dreams for sale

and these here

be your dreams

I Learned To Say Your Name

I learned to say your name

in my sleep

practiced the proper

pronunciation

before anyone taught

me of abc's

you didn't appear

in my dreams

I think I met you

in the clouds or a rainbow

or somewhere in my childhood

in moments creating

my favorite memories

it must have been fate

whispering in my ear

I learned to say your name

in my sleep

even in the earliest dreams

there were no scenes or moving parts

just paint brushes, varied colors of oils

an easel, a blank canvas and heaven

there was a series of questions posed

I never thought of answering

the sky asked what did I want

I only knew I wanted you

they told me to paint

the picture perfect

but no one could

what if there were no titles

paint a perfect picture

without seeing how

the perfect picture

looked when painted perfectly

I only knew I wanted you

I learned to say your name

in my sleep

not for sure how that happened

never heard of such an occurrence

I am sure you came

from somewhere

sent here just for me

got me repeating things I've said before

but didn't know their true meaning

like love you, forever, now and always

cherubim's must have sang your name

in times before

or you were music in another language

could have been notes to a song

only the angels know the words to

I believe you were waiting

for me to wake up

or dream, or wish, or pray, or hope

I learned to say your name

in my sleep

practiced the proper pronunciation

before anyone taught me of abc's

if wishes came true

you would be a frozen evening in August

under the blistering Texas sun

a perfect tan sweetened cup of coffee

arriving in the first of my mornings

there are days I stop, and pray for guidance

only to be reminded by birds and the wind

you were sent here just for me

I learned to say your name

in my sleep

it rolls out of my mouth pure love

when I'm awake, or when I sing

or kneel, or close my eyes to pray

didn't understand the concept of together

until each day missing you

becomes unbearable

and each day missing you, missing us

is always unbearable

I learned to say your name

in my sleep

it is the sweetest sound, I have ever heard

I am sure you came from somewhere

sent here just for me

got me repeating things I've said before

but didn't know their true meaning

like I will love you forever

you taste like always and eternity

you feel perfect now and always

I am sure you came from somewhere

I do believe you were sent here

just for me

what if there were no titles

Note To Self

when you start

to question yourself

examining your priorities

will leave you with more questions

I have questions still being birth

this mind is a canal of refuse

of new beginnings

and terrible endings

it is not up to me to know

where thoughts come from

where thoughts go

when you lose them

I've lost questions

I was going to ask myself

I had plans of answering

if I could remember the questions

sometimes questions

are not questions at all

they are points of knowledge

to start a quest to the unknown you

to write to

to write through

every answer

will be right and wrong

in the same instant

go ahead ask me something

please don't

this is not about your questions

it is a self-analyzation

a quiz of un comfortability

none of my questions appear

with logic included

do not try and make sense

answer the best you can

we still have questions

about the big bang

if there was a big bang at all

we are still curious

where rain comes from

why meteorologist keep their job

they seldom predict

the unpredictable

or why hurricanes have names

and tornadoes are called tornadoes

I would ask you a question

knowing you don't have the answer

stop asking of others

questions meant for you

to discover the solutions

you have no idea their source

don't know how they

typed it in the search engine

what version of dictionary used

if the origin of the words

had an origin at all

I write in questions

asked by these fingers

what if there were no titles

not knowing

where they come from

but answer anyway

stranger things

have happened

I keep writing

as though I know

even my answers

birth new questions

you must arrive

at the point of

understanding, this world

was formed of answers

scientist couldn't find

questions for

faith is believing

you don't need answers

questions, or knowing to move

you only need to keep moving

it's not up to me to know

where thoughts come from

or where thoughts go

when you lose them

I've lost questions

I was going to ask myself

and had plans of answering

if I could remember

where on my tongue

I hid the questions

The Word

I told my sons

the gifts, the talents

you have are not yours to keep

they are actual gifts

given you to refine

the process and procedure

for you to help others

you must put them to good use

I wrote a letter to myself

from one of me's to me

didn't know which one

to address it to

or give credit for sending

it read:

to all who reside here

there is so much left

to get done - to do

we must all do our part

if dreaming, writing and purpose

are the reasons we are here

write for the wishes

that never came true

for the love you gave

to unworthy participants

who were not ready

to receive or give love in return

those who believed hearts

were a secure vault

what if there were no titles

in the bank of emotions

the more you saved

the more dividends you would receive

with a higher rate of interest

all who thought time

would cease moving and wait

write for the love you received

and didn't know how to give back

write because a voice only knowing silence

loaned you their story to tell

write the stories of which

you are afraid to take ownership

pen all of the truths before now

you were terrified to write

write because it's your job

your purpose to do so

write because one day

there will only be words

unattached to pens or pages

you find sitting in front of you

some of the thoughts you possess

won't have enough courage

to dress for a proper introduction

they will not look presentable

you will not have the strength

to clothed them

although your hands will know

they must be preserved for histories sake

write because heaven told you to write

because you still have breath

write because others don't have faith

and refuse to create sound

use your voice to amplify

something worth listening to

write as proof

the shortest distance

between two thoughts is a poem

we read in the beginning was the word

but no one was there

to write them down

write as if right now

is the beginning

I told my sons to write

it doesn't have to be a poem

story, song or rap

write because you have fingers

or you are in love or out of love

in pain or full of laughter

write to prove to yourself

you can or you can't

write a letter to you from you

tell yourself something you forgot

or need to remember or need to forget

if dreaming, writing and purpose

are the reasons we are here

write for purpose - write for dreams

write because the reason you are here

is to write

Writing 101

when writing a poem

forget it's your fingers caressing the pen

adjust your grip loosely to the aft of its tip

remove your chest plate

bring your heart to skins edge

give it a chance to breathe

make sure you've set aside enough time

this sacrifice can't be given

if you're in a rush

in your eyes - this poem

will never stop trying to rewrite itself

you will be convinced it is a novel

hiding in the first syllables of an haiku

do not begin carving your thoughts

in favorite notebook

erasing becomes impossible

when you are too familiar with the pages

do not wish for tomorrow

or hold yesterday in plain sight

keep them at least

an arms distance in front of you

it will be much heavier to carry

if you are not prepared in advance

lay your emotions flat

use what every you have available

to scrub away the texture

keep a towel or rather towels close by

feelings often contain

more moister than first thought

use your feet as a unit of measurement

mark where you stand

take about four paces to your right

place your pain and your happiness

at a space of approximately

five feet apart - sometimes further

it will be of importance

to make a mental notation

of the person who conjured

said scribbling's... do not!

I repeat do not speak their name out loud

do not write it in the corners of your mind

force your eyes to remain open

it is the only way you can stop

their face from appearing

keep their name and any likeness of them

away from this poem

let this one be not for you personally

but of the consequence of loving

know beforehand

all is too big to fit in any of these lines

keep your broken parts whole

they have a tendency to leak

floods are easy to start

but difficult to stop

touch your pain and your happiness

slightly with brief strokes

they only matter to you

what if there were no titles

do not let them connect

the static gets stronger

the more time you spend petting them

tell them in your most demonstrative voice

to stay… stay!

do not give in

they will plead their case

in silence only you can translate

some words can't bare the weight

of sound, of memory

do not surrender to the impending

army of emotions

time stopped at your first kiss

push it forward

force time to move

nature is not responsible

for your changing of seasons

storms will come whether you are ready or not

there are no nurses or doctors

for the casualties of love

when writing a poem

there will be no point you understand

why it must be written

no one will know, this was all you had left of you

they won't care… some won't be listening

the applause won't be for what you think it's for

when writing a poem, remember

most people will think it was just a poem

bow gracefully… and let them

In Slumber

I grew up hearing

the human body

requires eight hours

of sleep to rejuvenate

my body moves

with the earth as it spins

I sleep when it asks me to rest

got too much day to chase

eight full hours would have me

in last place and this isn't a race

if the mind never sleeps

how can the body neglect it for that long

I wake rushing to pen thoughts

unaware pausing would not

allow me to catch up

I think it's a game to them

thought's I mean

they appear in glimpses

dancing, happy to have arrived

if I don't pay attention

they will gladly leave the same way

I believe they don't care who catches them

they just want to exist

want someone to pay attention

now they have me sleepless

waiting on their arrival

it is not that I miss sleep

I wish thoughts would stay longer

what if there were no titles

give me the opportunity

to fully clothe them

before they run off to visit someone

not ready to listen

I used to care what the listener

thought of my penability

that was before I understood

they probably get a full eight hours

of sleep before reading

and wouldn't understand the urgency

even if the message was in blood

they wouldn't get it

and I can't wait for them to

I didn't write it because I wanted to

because I thought it would

grab their conscious

tug slightly on their humanity

shake them, render them restless

I wrote it because I sat there

waiting on thoughts to pass by

snatched them out of the lineup

these were for me - if not

why did they pass so close

I write now because I have to

I always write in the now

of past, present and future now's

there are no moments other

than those we share right now

you can write five years ago

or two days from now

whatever you write or wrote

will appear in the right now

or should that be write now

as if the only thing

of consequence - is the now

I don't miss sleep

I don't think

sleep misses me

it used to visit

sporadically anyway

never stayed for long

so I stopped bidding it welcome

only invite it to pass through

when this body asks me

we have an understanding

me and sleep

if I could just get time to tag along

we would be a great threesome

time doesn't stop for any one

it will keep running fast

like it's got somewhere to be

but for right now it is just two of us

me and my pen

sleep will stop by

only when needed

but eight hours

is too long a period

not to pay attention

what if there were no titles

My Life In Rhythm

this poem

is the third beat in four

we will never get to sixteen

words can't count no way

math ain't got nothing to do

with pain, love or struggle

we all struggle with pain and love

struggle would be division

if we knew anything

about mathematics

I got bass in my pen

drums in my thoughts

so this is music

less the horns and guitar riffs

you don't have to believe me

I can hear it even if you can't

I am the third beat in four

minus sixteen in eight

and this ain't got nothing

to do with mathematics

it is a song of hearts

a double beat in between

the ones you used to listening to

my pen counts the measures

while measuring the weight of days

there will be days heavier than others

you can't lift by yourself

sometimes time won't move fast enough

to get out of your own way

it will stand as the barricade

demanding you force

your way through

there are days

you will have to force

your way through

at least I got this music

to dance by

to sing to, to run with

you will have to run

to arrive on time

even though

no one announced

what time will be on time

I got these beats

I don't even count no more

my pen holds

the muscle memory of fingers

words appearing in the wind

before I write them down

and you think poeting

is the way poets carve indentations

on themselves - so not true

this is music from a different realm

the kind you must be familiar

with God to hear

I hear God talking

I am just a secretary taking dictation

what if there were no titles

that has never been able

to write fast enough

to get the whole message

don't think this is the whole message

I am still struggling to keep up

this poem is the third beat in four

we will never get to sixteen

words can't count no way

I got bass in my pen

drums in my thoughts

so this is music

a double beat in between

the ones you are used to listening to

you don't have to believe me

but I've been given

unbelievable shhh to do

so me and time

ain't friends no more

we don't even hang out

on good days

I got these beats

I'm am trying to score

the music to my life

so shut the hell up

and let me..

and a one, and a two

and a three and a four

a one, a two, a three, and a four

a one, two, three

Lost

love keeps trying

to force me

to lose myself in you

there are voices in my head

I've never heard before

you have awakened parts of me

that were dormant

the last three resurrections

the last four reincarnations

dust still covers

the surface of my memories

from the last internment

wish someone could explain

how this body gets permission

to return here

to search for you

investigate your footprints

look into the eyes of those

who had the pleasure

to gaze at your presence

question your ex-lovers

in an official lineup

they were not aware

of what you are

couldn't see you were

a blessing until too late

the loss left each of them

devastated

what if there were no titles

you could never imagine

how many miles

the number of breaths

this heart has loved

how many times

it sacrificed itself

hoping on my next arrival

if I couldn't locate you

if my nose failed to chase

the aroma of your smile

if these hands couldn't feel

their way through time

an adequate substitution

or replacement would suffice

knowing there is nothing

normal about you

you stand galaxies above average

each time I tried to give myself

I would catch myself

loving on a curve

losing count of the beats

can't recall which return this is

I have searched for you

my whole life

all of them

every time I was sent back

at least nine of them

I had to beg for approval

asked if it were possible

could I bring support

to help me find you

this refurbished heart

has been given authorization

wears an authentic stamp

bears the original seal

even death is jealous

of the amount of passes

the number of times

I came back from heaven for you

it took a lot of lives to discover

this heart loving anyone else

was only practice

and I've never been good

at practicing

love can bear witness

this heart is yours

has been since its first rhythms

the questions in your eyes

I would love to answer

but words

in the arena of emotions

are not worth

the wasting of breath

I have days I will give to you

plastered with maps

of all the places

my mind travels

wishing you were there

what if there were no titles

I've created an ocean of love

can't wait for you to swim in

love keeps demanding

I find myself in you

the parts of my soul

that abandoned this body

when you first arrived

each time I've returned

I am more you than me

there are no visions

of forever

just pictures of you

no thoughts of eternity

just memories of you

love asked me

for parts of this body

I know were not detachable

this smile I wear every morning

these hands I thought

were mine to keep

my thoughts

even the ones

I hid in secret

I asked love

is this far enough

how about now

I could never find

my way back

to me from here

The Moon

it must have been

in the early years of growth

while stumbling my way

through learning to talk

walk and adolescence

I think I discovered it during

the first quarter moon past harvest

or the second full moon

after a blistering autumn day

the relevance of moments seem

to change with each shape

I marveled at the moon

before I knew of lunar cycles

its competition with the sun

or Apollo missions

before I had any inkling of Neil's visit

it all began when I read

the moon was made of cheese

in some long ago fairytale

used to rest my imagination there

thought it was the farthest my mind could reach

there is something about thoughts

surrounded by darkness felt beautiful on its inception

we remember the good days when we were young better

than bad days when you are old

I liked it better than its nemesis

the sun was too loud upon arrival

ripping the sky with bruises

what if there were no titles

purple, red... a wide array of colors

it was too pretty to be gorgeous

too bright for eyes to gaze directly into

the moon was just right, close enough not to touch

but could keep my imagination

completely out of harm's way

I've spent most of my life standing in harm's way

always loving beaches of white sands and oceans

upon discovering the moon could force waves

to move pass shorelines - change the dancing of tides

what fool would not fall in love with the moon

watching it play hide and seek with stars

noticing how many planets travel light years

to be in the visual vicinity of its glow

I have heard it has performed its play, its duty

in earth's sky for over four million years

some say it is earth's child formed from impacts

others say it had such a violent beginning

pummeled by asteroids and dying stars

don't know how it learned silence

I do understand why they say

the face of the moon will always remain the same

even before it becomes whole or full

it takes twenty-seven days

to complete one revolution on its own axis

and twenty-seven days before we view its face full

glow enchantingly outstanding

it is never feast or famine just different seasons

for planting and harvesting

determined by the moon's dance

across a darkened sky

call it miracle or heaven sent

maybe it is just what heaven meant it to be

I fell in love with the moon years ago

when I believed it was made of cheese

before the cow leaped over its crescent edges

they say its craters were formed of lessons

teaching us to marvel at the grand canyons

faraway islands and oceanic volcanoes

why many attempt to conquer mountains

why our imagination feels safe so many miles away

we trust the distance while fearing the closeness

we blame the moon for werewolves as if they existed

for strange sounds echoing in the dark of night

we say it's the reason this year's crops

were plentiful or scarce we treat the moon

as a distant relative, blame it for the bad karma

wicked deeds and crazy antics performed

when its face is full

my relationship is personal

the moon and I are used to lonely

it is the lone satellite watching the earth turn

I stand alone most days gazing

as life rotates around me

some of my relationships

felt of stars too close but distant

we could stand together smiling in direct view

but were literally light years from love

what if there were no titles

often wondering how to navigate glowing bright

in the midst of the darkest of trials

I have learned little

from solar eclipses witnessed

so little from the blackest of storm clouds

to which the moon pays no attention at all

imagine your only job is to shine

through whatever obstacle

the galaxy catapults your way

some days even with the sun burning bright

will have a hundred percent chance of storms

sometimes your glow will not appear bright enough

to make your path clear

there will appear to be a few days

you will feel absent as though the sky

this life was too big to find me waiting

some moments will arrive containing too much pain

will be darker than the blackest black

too thick to be pierced by light

some of my days arrive less the happy

I've built of promise - missing the promises

I made while happy and I were friends

not that we are enemies but my moon lessons

have yet to make a formidable impact

grasping for the full lessons of clouds

but my hands aren't long enough

I have yet to discover how to glow

although the moon rest

just out of reach on my fingers

Support the Art and the Artist...

the struggle is real

Thank you for your support

Acknowledgements:

I would like to Thank Fate, Lessons, Time and Love **(when it worked and didn't work).** I want to Thank my mother for her patience and her never ending prayers. She believed in me when my faith was in repair. To Janean and Jahmal for listening to every poem in this book at least twice and maybe three times for good measure. To Faye Hanshaw for the conversation of encouragement when needed, for support and kind words after reading my words, she always found something good in the worst of times to add a smile to my days. Thanks to Troshell, my sister Jaque, Brother in Law Joe Lacy, Kimberly Johnson for her passion, to my sons all of them Nick, Tremel, Dominique, Alexander and Jimmie, oh yea Bredon too. Much Love forever to my daughters Shanttel, Shayla and Brittany. Thanks to Cheryl, Trina, Fredrick, Booker and Shirley Green, Jan Harmonica, Sherry Gipson- English. I would like to Thank all my friends past and present I don't believe in past friends they are all on my present list. Thank you for the role you played in helping with this project. To my sister Tracy and brother Jimmy Thank you also. Thanks to support from Priceless, Ester, Donna, Donya. Mother Craddock, Patrick, Barbara, Angela, Gwen, Alex, Marcus, Natasha, Will Richie, Melody Memories, A.P., Aisha, Deidre, Kas, J'Car Marie, Camille, Eddie Cane, Zach, Kimberly W., Kay, Annika, Alex F. A Thank you goes out to the poetry community in every state who welcomed me to make an appearance, to every open mic and Slam venue for giving the opportunity to speak and perform. Thank you for purchasing the book and your comments even if you didn't forward them to my email. Thank every one for their prayers and well wishes. I am honored and grateful for the reading of my thoughts. Thank you one and all I didn't mean to leave names off but its just one page and I am excited about the completion of this project. Thank you once again.

About The Author

Born Albert Jeffrey Houston, in Dallas, Texas, the middle child of Jimmie Jay and Birdie Lee Houston. His father was born October 7, 1928 and laid to rest on September 26, 2001. When asked when did he discover or start writing? the answer doesn't change but it never comes attached to a date or year. So the answer *"all of his life"* has to suffice. When the question... when did he become serious about writing? He would tell the story of having two distinct types of poetry... some for sharing and the other just for self or personal. And how once at a gathering the stacks got mixed up and after moments of utter shock the response from the readers were life changing. There is no such thing as poetry just for self, or situations to be ashamed of. This life of filled with shared experiences and writing them down is the perfect way to help someone unaware of the possibility helping through problematic trials is available or they may be in need of answers to a situation you wrote as an experience. He believed some of the best writers didn't find writing serious enough or treated it a necessary daily activity until some revelation made them aware it was right there besides breathing and bathing. His morning mantra is: *"today I will write the best I know how but tomorrow I am positive my words will be better"*. He is most excited when working with youth not that he feels he can teach them but more so what he will gain and learn from the experience. There is much simplicity and complexity in one word, exploring the depths of discovery is a humbling endeavor. He writes every day in hopes of getting better. There isn't the possibly of becoming perfect only the accomplishment of learning to be efficient at thinking clearer.

what if there were no titles

Contact Information:

njalphabets.org

www.twitter.com/ajwordartist

www.facebook.com/ajhouston

www.youtube.com/ajhouston

www.reverbnation.com/ajhouston

poetajhouston@gmail.com

Additional Products:

<u>CD's</u>   Love Seasons - The Awakening - Whispers

<u>Coming Soon Books</u>

The Legend of Shrenk

Not Yet Lost

F.A.C.E. June 2016
(Fibromyalgia Awareness Changes Everything)

The Fireplace

Talking With Angels

Lost Pens
(A Pocket Guide for Writers)

<u>T-Shirts</u>

Poetic Lessons

NJA Gear

Poet's Supporting Hunger

For Booking: *Contact*

AJ Houston

@ poetajhouston@gmail.com

www.ingramcontent.com/pod-product-compliance
Lightning Source LLC
Chambersburg PA
CBHW060104170426
43198CB00010B/767